all for my children

all for my children

Sally Faulkner

with James Knight

hachette
AUSTRALIA

Published in Australia and New Zealand in 2016
by Hachette Australia
(an imprint of Hachette Australia Pty Limited)
Level 17, 207 Kent Street, Sydney NSW 2000
www.hachette.com.au

10 9 8 7 6 5 4 3 2 1

National Library of Australia
Cataloguing-in-Publication data:

Faulkner, Sally, author.
All for my children/Sally Faulkner.

ISBN: 978 0 7336 3727 8 (paperback)

Faulkner, Sally.
Mothers of kidnapped children – Australia – Biography.
Parental kidnapping.
Custody of children – Australia.
Custody of children – Lebanon.

Other Creators/Contributors: Knight, James, author.

362.8297092

Cover and picture sections design by Christabella Designs
Text design by Bookhouse, Sydney
Typeset in 12/19pt ITC New Baskerville by Bookhouse, Sydney
Printed and bound in Australia by McPherson's Printing Group

The paper this book is printed on is certified against the Forest Stewardship Council® Standards. McPherson's Printing Group holds FSC® chain of custody certification SGS-COC-004121. FSC® promotes environmentally responsible, socially beneficial and economically viable management of the world's forests.

This book is for Lahela, Noah and Eli.
Mummy loves you to the moon and back.

And to all those living through the waking
nightmare that is life after parental alienation –
I pray you can hold onto hope and memories of your
children, because they will get you through.

Contents

Author's note

If only. Two words we all hope never to say. If only. Two words I have said too many times.

If someone had told me when I first met Ali Elamine how our relationship would unfold I never would have believed it. Surely no one could apparently hate their partner so much? There are thousands of parents in similar circumstances, kept apart from the children they love, who can understand the emotions involved. No amount of tears will fill the emptiness a mother or father carries for the child they can't hold close. I would never wish this situation upon anyone, even my worst enemy. I would never have denied contact to Ali.

When you love someone as much as I do Lahela and Noah, and then have all access to them blocked, you would risk everything for them. I know this is true, because I did exactly that. And lost them.

After not being able to see, or even speak, to my children for ten months, I was desperate. I tried everything and continually called, emailed and Skyped Ali but was barred from making contact. The last time I'd been allowed to speak to Lahela and Noah I heard such sadness in their voices. They were in Beirut but wanted to come home. I had to console them while hiding the fact my own heart was breaking.

Everything I have done, and continue to do, is for my children, for Lahela and Noah. I have gone through the courts, begged government departments to help, reached out to the media and flown across the world to see them again. Many people have an opinion about me and the actions I have taken, but they don't know my story; they don't know all that has happened and they aren't living with the constant aching loss, the knowledge that my children should be able to see both their parents.

Long after the media has forgotten about me, Lahela and Noah, my children will still be living in a place they don't want to be, without one of their parents.

Neither Ali nor I are the true victims in all this. The only ones I feel sorry for are our beautiful children. They deserve better. Our children's voices should be louder than all the other noise.

The harsh reality is, I don't know when I will see my children again. Living with that knowledge every day is almost too hard. But I will never stop fighting to be with them again. I have written this book so that when Lahela and Noah are old enough they will know who I am and how we were separated. In the telling, there will be moments that aren't flattering to me or to Ali, but I can't change what has happened and I can't lie to them.

To Lahela and Noah: I'm sorry. I want you to know that none of this was ever my choice, none of this is your fault, and I never stopped trying to bring you home. I love you both, and will always love you. I hope one day I can tell you all this in person. Until then, this is our story.

Part I

Part I

Chapter One
Tuesday, 12 April 2016

The thunder sounded so different to the way it did in Brisbane. It was eerie. It echoed in the mountains behind Beirut and seemed so far away, yet so close. I curled myself up tighter under the blanket and moved around until my hips couldn't feel the concrete floor beneath the mattress. The floor was cold. The air was cold. I was very, very cold.

There was so much noise. Apart from the thunder, the stinking diesel generator in the corner banged away, and six of my seven cellmates did as they always did: talked and smoked. My seventh, on the mattress right alongside me, was the only one who had somehow drifted off. She was flinching but not waking. Tara Brown, one of the most recognised journalists in Australia. All glamour and dignity had been stripped from us both.

Finally, I fell asleep, only to be woken by yelling and wailing from men in a cell further along the block. Their torments saddened me. The poor men. I didn't know what was happening to them, and it was pointless to make assumptions. Assumptions wasted time and energy. It was best to clear my mind as much as possible and try to get a bit more sleep.

When morning came, I looked out our slit of a window and saw feet running through puddles. That was all. There were no faces. Just feet. And bits of legs. And mud. And puddles. The puddles were important to me because they were proof that it had rained quite heavily during the night, yet I hadn't heard it, which meant I must have slept. What a relief. But that's when the agony struck me. The sleep had been my escape, but now I was awake, and nothing had changed except for the puddles. Oh God, we were still in a grimy cell with a squat toilet, a tiny window and a bright light from a bulb above that never went out. Now, it was time for the nightmares to begin. Nightmares that only came when I was awake. Emotional and mental torture. Questions, so many questions.

How had I come to be here?

Maybe it was better to ask: How do I believe the unbelievable?

Chapter Two

When we are children we often don't see what our parents see. We are usually oblivious to the tensions in the air. At least, in my house, I was. I was too busy riding my bike with my friends in our cul-de-sac; or climbing my favourite tree in my grandparents' front yard; or dragging my pet mouse, Pepper, around in my little brother's toy speedboat. I loved that mouse. It was fat; it ate too much. And then the next-door neighbour's cat tried to eat it. We buried Pepper in the backyard and held a memorial service. All the neighbours, including the one who owned the cat, came to pay their respects. It was the first loss I'd experienced and I still remember how sad I felt.

But there were also many happier moments, such as when I won the occasional medal for figure-skating on rollerskates.

I still have some dodgy old photos of me in leotards: a 1990s girl thinking she was pretty cool. I played cricket too, and was a better bowler than most of the boys. I couldn't bat very well, though. I wasn't very good at riding a skateboard either, but at least I had a go. It was in my nature to always have a go. I was an outdoors girl who barely watched TV; I can't even remember the names of any cartoons I watched. But I know now that I didn't see the things that my parents saw.

When I was about seven, I had no idea the pressures that Mum and Dad were under. They'd just sold the family home in Albany Creek, in Brisbane's north-west, and had bought a block of land in the same suburb. They planned to build a house on it, and in the meantime we all moved into my maternal grandfather's home. Pa had been living by himself after Nanna passed away some years earlier. It was a bit of a squeeze, but it didn't bother me and the days went by without any real worries. Or so I thought.

Then came the night that changed our lives forever. It was dinnertime, and we were all sitting around the table when my brother, Simon, who was three years younger than me, started to whinge about eating his peas, and he accidently knocked a spoon out of Dad's hand. The peas went all over the floor. Suddenly Dad got up and walked out. And that was it. The marriage was over.

I was too young to understand the whys behind what had happened – of course their marriage didn't end because of spilt peas but as I've said, I was unaware of the stresses and strains Mum and Dad were going through; certainly nobody knew at that stage that Dad was unwell. His changing behaviour and intense moods were a symptom of an illness but it took a while to discover this. He was eventually diagnosed with water on the brain and he nearly died when he had surgery to rectify the problem.

For me, it was much easier to blame Simon, and for some time afterwards I resented my brother. He was the real cause, wasn't he? If only he had eaten his peas. Ridiculous, I know. Later, Mum sat Simon and me down and made sure we realised that the divorce wasn't our fault. It must have been so hard for her to do that so reassuringly. I don't remember how I felt – but I do remember a sadness.

'No matter what happens, Dad and I still love you both, and always will,' she said.

After the break-up, Simon and I stayed with Mum at Pa's place, and we went to Dad's, which was only a short drive away, at the weekends. Looking back now, few things remind me of visiting Dad more than toasted cheese sandwiches. Dad cooked them for us all the time. You know those Kraft singles wrapped in plastic? Dad put so much love into preparing those sandwiches; basically they were the only things he could cook, other than over-boiled vegetables that would fall apart as soon as we touched them. I think we all preferred the cheese toasties.

Mum and Dad were very different people, so I can see now why they didn't stay together. Dad, an electrician, was a little quirky. He could recite the periodic table, and would often go off on random bursts about some unexpected topic. I remember the day he lectured me about ants.

'The green ant might be bigger but if it goes into a black ants' nest it will get killed.'

Dad was full of what I thought was useless information and he shared all of that information, often. He always drove a white Holden Commodore station wagon. No matter what model he bought, it had to be white. Simon and I used to sit in the back and listen to him prattle on while we were on our way to some place or other. Space and aeronautics were two of his favourite topics, and Simon loved listening to everything he had to say. We'd be driving along, and I'd start to tune out to all the *blah-blah-blah*, while Simon hung on every word. It's not surprising that my little brother has grown up to become a helicopter engineer. I wish I'd listened a little more.

It's fair to say that Dad didn't have the greatest social skills, and he often preferred his own company to that of others. He wasn't the most demonstrably affectionate father, but I knew I could always count on him. He loved us in his own special way.

Mum, a primary school teacher, didn't have any unusual traits that I was aware of. She blended in. There was no fuss with her; she did what she had to do, day in, day out, which couldn't have been easy when she was the parent mostly responsible for her children's welfare and upbringing. I learned a lot by watching her. She treated everyone the same, and is a very considerate and caring person. I didn't realise how close we were until I moved away, and it wasn't until I became a mother that I truly appreciated our relationship. She has always been my best friend, the one person who can make me feel special, and she is always there when anything goes wrong. In turn, when she is having a bad day, she'd rather talk to me than anybody else. After Mum split with Dad, Simon and I used to have friendly arguments every now and then about favourites.

'Mum loves you better,' Simon would tease.

'And Dad loves you more,' I would reply.

In hindsight, we were kind of right. But these allegiances didn't affect us; we were raised by both parents with love, warmth and security. We were so lucky to have our grandparents too; they played a really big part in our upbringing. Whenever Mum was working, Pa would take us to school and pick us up in his little red Corolla. Simon and I never went to after-school care; one of our grandparents was always there. I have very clear memories of Pa. He was a strong-willed, old-fashioned man. A hard worker who loved a chat. On the other side of the family, Dad's father, Grandpa, who fought in World War II, was always the one to put Simon and me in our place if we mucked up; his bellowing voice was enough to intimidate any child. I can still hear his firm words at the dinner table whenever we forgot to say please or thank you.

'Remember your elephant,' he'd say.

What? I didn't know what an elephant had to do with good manners; I just accepted it was something that everyone said. It was only years later that I realised it was Grandpa's unique way of getting us to think about what we were doing and to get his message across. I loved all my grandparents dearly.

Despite Mum and Dad's break-up, I still had a sense of family and stability in my childhood. I felt safe. But now, looking back, maybe I settled for things in my own marriage because I didn't want to drop the peas.

I loved going to school, mostly because I was a sociable girl and I couldn't wait to be with my friends. I was an average student – I got Bs, never As or A+s – but if I'd applied myself more it could have been different. I cruised through primary and high school without many worries; there were certainly no raging-hormone moments in the teenage years, during which I saw my friends hate their parents and the whole world. Simon avoided that stage too. Neither of us got into much trouble, and I am sure we have Mum and Dad to thank for that. They'd shown great trust in us as they'd co-parented together ever since we were very young, and as we grew up we didn't want to break that trust. As a result, I'd like to think we matured into responsible teenagers. I can honestly say that Simon didn't get into even one fist-fight, which was quite an achievement for a teenage boy at the time. But it was a different matter for others.

One day, in Year 11, I was sitting with a group of friends when, suddenly, there was a loud rumble of feet running on concrete. I looked up and saw a lanky guy with long blond hair sprinting past, and telling another fifty or more students to follow him: 'Yeah, come on, come on.' My friends and I stayed where we were, but soon enough it seemed half the school had stampeded to a space near the library. Then there was a moment or two of quiet before we heard a lot of boys yelling, and sure enough that was followed by a number of teachers racing out of their staffrooms in a bid to stop a fight. That afternoon word spread that the blond-haired instigator was Brendan Pierce. Later, my best friend's mum warned us: 'You stay away from that boy. He's nothing but trouble.' Surprisingly, his dad was quite a high-ranking police officer in the area, and his mother was a nurse. They were lovely people, but Brendan was chaotic – back then. I had nothing to do with him at school and, in fact, I thought he was a bogan. I don't think any of those things now – but I'll explain that later.

Although I was a matter-of-fact schoolgirl, one thing happened in Year 12 that made me a little different from my friends. Again the revelation happened over a family dinner, this time with Lew, Mum's partner who had been living with us for quite a while. As we sat together eating and discussing the day, Mum stunned us all.

'I'm having a baby,' she said. I don't remember Mum seeming nervous telling us, she was just very happy.

My immediate reaction was to look at her and think to myself: *What, she still does it!* My surprise gave way to happiness for Mum, and when my little brother, Bryce, finally came along, I was thrilled. From when I was as young as ten and still playing with Barbie dolls, I dreamed of being a mother. I hoped it would be something that would happen to me when I was older. And the time I spent with Bryce only strengthened my desire. I loved hanging out with him. I'd come home from school and cuddle him on the lounge. He seemed so tiny in my hands, so precious and vulnerable.

Whenever I could, I took Bryce out so Mum could have some time to rest; most of the time it was wonderful, although I suffered my fair share of judgmental looks and comments from people who didn't know me. They saw a seventeen-year-old girl pushing a stroller along a street, or going into a grocery store with a baby on her hip, and jumped to conclusions. On one occasion I took Bryce to an indoor play centre, and I heard one of the mums purposely speak loud enough for me to hear: 'Oh, she's just *so* young.' I wanted to say something but I was too shy. I hated those automatic judgments from people without the full story (and I still do). It eventually got to the stage that whenever I was in public, I would talk to Bryce in very assured ways, like: 'Come here, little bro.' I was probably being silly, but so were the people passing comment in the first place. Their reactions were just some of those everyday lessons I learned while growing up.

The year after Bryce was born I left home for the first time. When I finished Year 12, I was accepted to study Applied Science at the university at Lismore on the far north coast of New South Wales. I had wanted to study teaching, but I messed up my university preferences and was offered this course first. It didn't really matter, though, because I had a strong interest in science and had done well in it at school, so I went with the flow (perhaps my dad's facts had rubbed off a little).

I was lucky because Mum had enough saved to buy an investment duplex in Lismore that I could live in while I was at uni, which meant I didn't have to pay rent. To help pay for food, bills and other costs I worked as a swim instructor, worked in a nightclub and did some babysitting. It all helped. And being on my own for the first time was exciting. I drank enough alcohol during that period to last a lifetime. I had never been a big drinker and definitely am not now, partly because I was diagnosed with Crohn's disease when I was about ten and partly because it just doesn't interest me, but these were my single, uni-student years, so I partied a bit. It wasn't as though I went completely mad, especially in comparison to most people in their late teens and early twenties. It was just a stage I went through. Again, it was another life lesson.

* * *

I enjoyed uni, and managed to keep ticking off the subjects until I had just two units to go in my third and final year. I returned to Brisbane with the intention of finishing my degree externally. However, when procrastinating over an assignment one evening, I got bored and started to look at job advertisements online. One caught my attention, and when I clicked on its link and began to read, I thought: *That job sounds pretty cool.* So, without thinking too much about what I was doing, I applied for a recruitment day that was going to be held in Brisbane. I answered page after page of questions, quite a few of which were based around moral dilemmas. The application took about an hour to finish, and then I sent it off and thought nothing more about it. Two weeks later, finishing my degree suddenly didn't seem important anymore.

Chapter Three

It was a Saturday morning, late 2006, and about 300 candidates had turned up at an office building near Brisbane
airport. We were ushered into a big room and addressed by
two women. I couldn't believe what was happening. Here
I was, among so many others, hoping to be chosen as a
flight attendant for one of the most prestigious airlines in
the world, Emirates. We watched a promotional video about
the lifestyles of attendants. It all looked so glamorous: the
glitz of Dubai, where Emirates was based; the shots of stunning people wearing immaculate uniforms and gliding like
superstars through airports. I had only one thought: *I don't
care what it takes, I'm going to be an air hostess.*

At some point I said hi to the girl sitting next to me. Her
name was Sacha, and she was from the Gold Coast. At first,

I was nervous around her because she seemed so confident and she just kept talking, but as the day went on, we both relaxed and enjoyed each other's company. After lunch we were all back in the big room with two officious women who had such strong English accents there was no chance of ever mistaking where they were from. They called us up one by one to receive our résumés and to conduct a thirty-second interview. Not much can be said in that space of time, but the women obviously knew what they were looking for. I can only remember answering two questions: 'What is your current job?' and 'Do you have any visible tattoos or birthmarks?' After everyone had been through, we were told that those who reached the next stage of the application process would be contacted by five o'clock that afternoon.

Sacha and I swapped phone numbers before we went on our own ways. I was at home when, right on 5pm, I received a message from Sacha. She had been chosen. I'd heard nothing, so a little bit of jealousy crept in. I kept hoping I'd get the call, so I didn't reply straightaway. By 6.30pm I was still waiting, and Mum tried to comfort me.

'Don't worry,' she said. 'You're in a good position. You're so close to finishing uni, so concentrate on that.'

'But Mum, I *really* want that job.'

Just as I said that, my phone rang. It was an unknown number.

'Is that Sally Faulkner?' said a woman with an English accent.

'Yes.'

'We'd like to see you at nine tomorrow morning for an interview, please.'

I texted Sacha. I was no longer jealous.

The next morning we met again. Sacha was chirpy, bouncing from place to place, and smiling all the time. There were about 100 other hopefuls. The day was intense: interviews, psychological tests, more moral-dilemma scenarios, in and out of offices, more tests, more interviews. Bit by bit, people were culled. By late afternoon there were only forty of us left.

We returned the following day for more interviews, and more culling. By the end, only seven candidates remained. Sacha and I were among them, but we still didn't know our fate.

'We'll call you tomorrow if you've been accepted,' the Emirates representative said as she dismissed us.

I tossed and turned a lot that night. But in the morning, the phone rang and I was given the news I so desperately wanted to hear: I was in. So was Sacha. But then, as it turned out, I wasn't there yet. In the following weeks I had to submit endless pages of paperwork, which included a comprehensive medical report that had to be completed by my doctor.

'I think you might have a problem,' he told me. 'There's a question about Crohn's disease.'

Crohn's is a chronic inflammatory bowel disease that can vary from mild to severe, and when I was ten I had been so sick with it that I ended up in hospital. When I was in Year 12 I'd had another really bad run with it, and had lost a lot of weight. Now, although I was feeling healthy and seemed to be in a remission phase, I had no idea how Emirates would react. I felt robbed. After all I'd been through, one of the very last questions I had to answer in the whole application process was going to ruin my chances.

I worried for about two weeks – until I received an email with an airline ticket to Dubai.

I left Brisbane in February 2007. Mum and Dad both came to say goodbye at the airport. When they saw the six other new recruits, all beautifully made up and walking like models in flowing dresses, Mum looked at me in my jeans and singlet and said, 'Don't worry, you'll be right. You've got this far.'

I felt like Plain Jane, but on the flip side, I was so excited. I was twenty-one years old and about to start an incredible adventure. I'd never been outside Australia – a holiday to Tasmania with Mum and Simon was as far as I'd ever been – so to find myself on a plane heading to a far-off, mystical place that I knew so little about was surreal, to say the least. It helped that Sacha was with me. We were in this together. And so were the five others, including one woman, Rachel, who kept us entertained just by being herself.

'So, where *is* Dubai, anyway?' she asked just after we'd boarded and were looking at a flight map. 'What's it like there?'

Someone answered: 'I don't really know, but there's a lot of desert there.'

We were all pretty naïve. Just young women who were working out who we were, where we wanted to go, and what we wanted to do with our lives.

Sixteen hours later we touched down, and were soon on a bus heading towards our living quarters. I couldn't stop smiling. I looked through the windows and realised that the promotional videos I'd seen didn't tell the full story. There was more hustle and bustle on the streets, and a lot more dust.

I was lucky enough to be paired with Sacha in a brand-new spacious two-bedroom apartment in Sharjah, which I thought was a pretty grimy part of the city. From our third-floor windows we could see other concrete buildings; a few mosque minarets pointing to the sky; and a dusty, murky haze blanketing the distance. At ground level were trip hazards every few steps on poorly aligned footpaths – and rubbish. Rubbish was everywhere: on the paths, on the streets, but not on the lush green gardens that were distinct all over the city because they were so perfectly manicured.

From memory, we only had two days to acquaint ourselves with our new home, and get over any jet-lag, before we started six weeks of training at a state-of-the-art facility near the airport. There was so much to learn: configurations of different aircraft; emergency procedures; safety checks; arming and dis-arming doors of different types of aircraft; pre-flight service; preparing and serving trays; how to manoeuvre the carts; and how to address passengers. We even spent about four days being taught about make-up, grooming and how we were to wear our uniforms. After her comment at the airport, I think Mum would have been relieved to know that.

There was little downtime. Most training classes began at about 7am, and we didn't make it back to our apartment until 7pm. Then we had to study what we'd learned during the day to make sure we were ready for an exam the next morning. It was an exhausting schedule, five days a week, and I spent most of those first weekends resting up and cramming as much information as I could. Trainees had come from many different countries. Some found the pace really difficult, especially those who didn't speak English as their first language, because all classes were conducted in English. However, there were others who could speak six or more languages fluently. They were incredible women and men and I was slightly in awe of them.

After cramming in so much, I was relieved when the six weeks were finally over and it was time to begin my six-month probationary period in the air. I can't recall much about my first flight – it was a quick turnaround to Muscat, about forty-five minutes away – but the second flight, to somewhere in India, had the worst turbulence I was ever to experience. The attendants had to sit down for most of the trip, but still it was decided that we had to provide some type of meal service. It was very rushed, and even as we were coming in to land we were frantically cleaning up. The trash compactor was so full that we had to put some rubbish into a gigantic bag that we then shoved into a toilet. A few other bags were tossed in there as well – when we landed, the toilet door nearly fell off because of all the weight pushing forward on it. Other rubbish fell on the floor at the back of the main cabin. It was all a bit of a disaster, really, and made me wonder if this sort of thing happened all the time.

Thankfully, things improved, although my first roster was a nightmare. It was just turnaround after turnaround. Say, for example, a return trip to Beirut: we would spend nearly four hours in the air, then after landing we would wait on the aircraft while catering and cleaning services were managed, before we would take off and fly back. Technically I visited quite a few countries, but staring at them through a little window while taxiing on a tarmac was normally nothing to get excited about, although I must admit I was thrilled when I flew over the Giza pyramids and into Cairo for the first time.

I was even more excited when I got my first layover. Not surprisingly it was to London, because Emirates had a number of flights to Heathrow every day. But I actually didn't spend much time playing the tourist; I was still coming to terms with whizzing from one destination to the next, and by then I was feeling homesick and just wanted to spend time with Mum. I finally got the chance to do that after my probation had finished and I was allowed a trip home. It was great to see my family and friends but, tellingly, after a few days I had the overwhelming urge to leave again. Why? Because I stayed at home and watched all my mates go off to nine-to-five jobs, and at that time I couldn't think of anything worse. It was only then that I realised why I'd originally trawled the Internet for jobs: I was scared to finish uni and be forced into a mundane lifestyle. I wanted to see the world.

And now I was.

I returned to Dubai with renewed energy. I wanted to see more of the world, so I applied for a position on the huge A380s, which required their own specially trained crews. I was accepted, and now I really was up and flying. New York was the best layover: I was paid good money to have a week off while staying in some of the best downtown hotels. And then there was the shopping. The first time I walked into Abercrombie & Fitch I couldn't believe it: there were all these handsome guys – models, no doubt – parading around without shirts on. Oh my goodness. I went in not intending to buy anything but I left with bags and bags of clothes. I just couldn't help myself because these guys would come up to me and say: 'Would you like me to try this on for you?' I mean, what was I meant to do? I even bought clothes for Simon, and I never buy clothes for my brother. Thankfully there was nothing small enough for Bryce, otherwise I really would have broken my bank. On the same trip, I ice-skated at the Wollman Rink in Central Park. It was Christmas time, and the rink was so crowded I could barely move, but what did that matter? It was one of those precious moments I will remember forever.

That first Christmas with Emirates was wonderful. I often worked behind the bar on the A380s, and on Christmas Day I stuck up a little tree, which most of the crew were able to gather round to exchange presents. Emirates might have been a big corporate power, but its flight crews were very family-oriented. We were also very social; more often than not whenever we landed for a layover we'd go back to our hotel, then meet later for a drink, dinner or a night out. But being social did have its traps. There were more than a few times when I was with a crew being briefed before a flight when suddenly an awkward silence would descend as the captain or first officer walked in; it didn't take much imagination to realise that someone might have enjoyed being overly social at a recent party, get-together or layover.

And that leads me to the behaviour of some of the passengers. Yes, the mile-high club is not a myth. I've had a captain say to me: 'The cameras are picking up a couple having sex in first class. Can you tell them to stop?'

On another occasion as I was serving pre-flight drinks, a passenger grabbed my arm and asked: 'Excuse me, why is there a tiny human underneath the plane. We're flying so fast how can he hang on?'

'Sir, that's a member of the ground staff. We haven't taken off yet.'

The passenger then started to speak really loudly, drawing the attention of others. I told him to calm down, and to put his suitcase away.

'I'm afraid I can't serve you a drink,' I said.

'I'm not drunk. I just thought we'd be there by now.'

Yes, we were never far away from a wacky moment or two. One of my colleagues was one of the main sources of humour. She once put hundreds of teabags in her bath because her grandmother told her it was a good way to get a tan. She succeeded only in making herself dizzy, and when she stepped out of the bath she passed out on the floor and took a while to recover.

Being a flight attendant is one of those rare jobs that allows you to see the full range of human behaviour and emotions. When I had some downtime in Dubai, I was witness to a vast cross-section of life. Sharjah was an eye-opener for someone raised in the Brisbane suburbs. I saw good and bad on the streets, but a couple of things really bothered me. I was sickened by the frequent sounds of men clearing their throats and spitting – sometimes right next to me; and there were other moments when, even though I covered up, I would get a creepy look from someone passing by. As a result, I often didn't venture out far unless I was going in a taxi to areas I felt safer in, such as the centre of Dubai or shopping districts on Sheikh Zayed Road.

The most confronting experience, though, was witnessing what I could only consider to be the slavery of Indian, Pakistani and Bangladeshi workers who were piled onto buses in scorching heat and taken to work for long hours on high-rise building sites. They looked so sad and defeated. I heard stories of workers who had killed themselves because they thought they had no way out, and they hoped that some sort of insurance payout might help their families. I've looked online for Dubai 'before and after' photos; the growth in the past twenty years has been incredible, and so much of that is because of the poor workers who were paid a pittance to build the city. It still doesn't sit well with me. But I must admit – and it shames me now – that I initially didn't think too much about their situation because I was blinkered by the glamour of Dubai: all the glitzy towers, the wealth and the pumping social scene.

Dubai is an adults' playground. Beach parties, house parties, nightclubs – there was always something amazing going on. Like so many of my workmates I fell into that ex-pat lifestyle. I was in my early twenties, a long way from home and determined to make the most of what was on offer. There was never a shortage of good-looking men willing to help us have a great time: ex-pat and local high-rolling businessmen who would buy us drinks and food all night. Most of them knew how to turn on the charm; they rarely left without phone numbers, which would lead to dinner dates in extravagant restaurants, no expense spared. Sometimes when I gave out my number I wouldn't hear any more for a couple of weeks, and then a bunch of flowers would be delivered to my apartment or I'd answer a phone call and hear: 'Hey, it's [so-and-so]. Remember me? Do you want to go out for a drink?' One friend, who used to work for Emirates but had since taken another job in Dubai, picked me up one afternoon in a Porsche four-wheel drive.

'It's new. Would you like to drive it?' he asked.

Without any thought about licences or road rules, I got behind the wheel and drove further into a way of life that was far removed from Albany Creek.

The most outrageous days of all started with someone, normally an Emirates friend or two, saying: 'Let's have brunch.' Usually that brunch would turn into drinks well into the afternoon, then clubbing and more drinks that night, and a hangover that was best cured by lazing by the pool on top of someone's apartment block. Work and play could blend dangerously together. My ultimate lack-of-sleep record was the time I got off a long flight, immediately went partying, then slept on a beach and got so sunburned that I couldn't lie down properly, but I still had to keep going and keep working on a turnaround shift. I finally returned home exhausted but then spent hours throwing up before I was taken to hospital. I was diagnosed with a virus; it was my own fault after having only two hours' sleep in three days. It was no wonder I was so run-down.

I did some silly things during those years. Actually, crazy is a better word. Remember MySpace, one of the first social-networking sites? One evening I received a friend request from a man named Jonathan in Dallas, Texas. We kept in touch for about a year before we switched our 'friendship' to Facebook and after a while swapped phone numbers so we could call and text each other, and we Skype-called as well. This went on for quite a few months until Jonathan invited me to visit him. I was reluctant at first, but he convinced me when he said he was a police officer and would send me a picture of his ID. So, swept away by the mystery, sense of adventure and an irresistible American accent, I booked a staff travel ticket and away I went. Jonathan picked me up at the airport. He had a really warm smile and was friend-lier than I'd imagined him to be, so this made me feel comfortable with my decision to go. Nevertheless, it was still weird to meet a man I'd never met, so to speak. We got along well and were both keen to see what would happen between us. I stayed in a hotel, and on the second day, after shaking off the jet-lag, I got dressed up to be taken out to dinner. Now, this is where things got interesting. Minutes after Jonathan picked me up, a car side-swiped us and nearly ran us off the road. It sped off and Jonathan went into action straightaway.

'We've got to get them!'

He put his foot down and we sped off into a scene that could have been straight out of a Hollywood movie. I hung on for dear life, thinking: *We're going to crash, I'm going to die, and Mum doesn't even know where I am.* I'd been too afraid to tell her that I was going halfway across the world to meet a stranger with a cool accent.

The chase continued until we got to a car park at the back of a dirty, dingy motel. It was dark, no streetlights at all. The other car had stopped just ahead of us.

'Stay where you are,' Jonathan told me as he opened his glove box and pulled out a handgun.

I could only think the worst: I was going to witness someone getting shot. What the hell had I gotten myself into? I was a little shaky, and held back a nervous laugh.

The front doors of the other car opened, and two men got out.

Jonathan, who was pointing his gun at the men, yelled over his shoulder to me: 'Call for back-up.'

I scrambled round looking for my phone.

'What's the number?' I asked.

'Nine-one-one.'

'Where are we?'

'Find out.'

Against my better judgment, I got out of the car and started to look for any sort of street sign or address. I walked onto a grassed area, and felt my heels sink into the ground. Suddenly I fell over. I got back up and then a sprinkler system turned on. I was soaking within seconds.

'What are you doing?' yelled Jonathan.

Finally, I got through on the emergency number. I was half-screaming, half-laughing; I think I was a little hysterical.

'Calm down, ma'am. Please calm down,' said the operator.

'I'm okay. I'm sorry I'm laughing.'

'We take these calls seriously, ma'am. What is happening?'

I explained the situation as well as I could, but I still didn't know where we were.

'Can you find out, ma'am?'

By now, Jonathan had the two men lying facedown with their hands outstretched.

I ripped off my shoes, and walked around the nearest corner and saw a homeless man sitting among a pile of blankets.

'Excuse me, do you know what street this is, please?'

He lifted his head, stared through me, and then put his head down again to sniff some paint. I quickly moved on. Behind me I heard Jonathan yelling at the two men: 'Stay down, just stay down!'

I walked a little further and saw a street sign. Thank goodness.

Minutes later two police cars screamed to a stop and some officers arrested the men we'd chased. It turned out that they were illegal immigrants and their car was unregistered, which was why they'd taken off like they had. Jonathan felt he had done the right thing, and was very pleased with himself. He then apologised and asked if I'd still like to go for dinner.

'I don't think so. Look at me, I'm a drowned rat.'

We decided to get some takeout, and as we were driving away I began to laugh uncontrollably. Welcome to Dallas. Would anyone ever believe me? I stayed for a fortnight but realised the relationship wouldn't go any further because Jonathan seemed married to his work. He didn't take any time off while I was there, and I only got to see him after he'd finished his shifts.

I went back to Dubai, and on one of my regular calls home I told Mum about Jonathan, the trip and the crazy chase. She reacted as any devoted mother would, and I promised I would never do anything as reckless as that again.

As time passed, I quietened down, and eventually I preferred to hang out at friends' places to watch movies and chat; or just turn on the air conditioning, draw the curtains and sleep for twelve hours between flights. Looking back, I wouldn't change anything about the lifestyle. It was fun. I was young, and I never did anything I am ashamed of. I worked hard too and after a while I had saved enough money to buy a Brisbane apartment with Mum. I was proud of that. And thanks to the staff travel perks, I was able to fly Mum, Simon and Bryce over for a quick visit to London and a two-week holiday in the Seychelles, and I got Dad over to Bangkok, Dubai and Oman. They were good times. I didn't think hard about my future; I was content to live in the moment and see where that took me.

And then I met Ali.

Chapter Four

It is funny how one decision can change your life. You know those sliding-door moments that at the time seem insignificant but turn out to be anything but. I didn't know it then, but one phone call in July 2008 would end up shaping everything to come. I was tired. Only hours earlier I had returned to Dubai after a long flight, and I wanted to catch up on some sleep. But Sacha called to invite me to a house party. She had moved out and I was living on my own, so I was looking forward to a bath and bed. She always knew how to twist my arm, though: 'Please come, it'll be fun.'

I got there a short time later and looked around the room for Sacha. She hadn't yet arrived. About half the people there were from Emirates, the rest were other ex-pats and their local friends. It was a typical party: crowded, loud music, plenty of alcohol. The first person I noticed was standing in a corner near a makeshift bar. He really stood out, dressed like a teenage surfer dude: tanned, goofy, afro hair, skater shoes, long socks, cargo board shorts and a T-shirt. The guy next to him wore the standard party clothes: dressy shirt and trousers. They both looked at me, but we didn't exchange hellos.

I looked around the room again and didn't see anyone I knew. Then I looked back at the guy with the afro; I thought he seemed different, kind of out of place, really. I went to get a drink at the bar, but it was a tight squeeze because the surfer guy wouldn't move away. I wondered if he was doing it on purpose.

'Excuse me!' I shouted over the hubbub of the room.

'Oh, sorry, I didn't see you there.'

In the jostle of the bar I accidentally spilled some vodka on his shoes and shorts. I was very apologetic, and embarrassed, but he made a joke that I didn't hear above the music.

'Don't worry about it,' he then said in a really attractive Californian accent. 'Hey, you're going red!'

It was obvious that he and his friend had already downed many drinks. As I moved away I saw the front door open, and was pleased to see Sacha. We caught up on each other's news and then she asked me if I'd met her new boyfriend, Ed.

'No, I don't know who he is.'

'He's over there in that corner.'

'Near the bar?'

'Yes.'

'Oh no!'

I explained to Sacha what had happened.

'It's all right,' she assured me. 'Surfer guy's not my boyfriend. He's Ed's flatmate. He seems nice.'

We walked over to them, and surfer guy grinned: 'Hey, it's the vodka girl.' His hair and clothes didn't hide who he was: he was a surfer, skater, goofball guy. Not my normal type – I was usually attracted to tall, rugged, handsome guys – but there was something appealing about him: he was charismatic, obviously a joker and he gave out a really friendly, approachable vibe. I wasn't, however, so taken with him that I felt the need to know him better. We chatted for a while, and then I walked off and met some other people. Towards the end of the night, I went to the bathroom, and when I came out, there was surfer guy standing right in front of me.

'Do you need the bathroom?' I asked.

'No, I just wanted to see where you were.'

As I squeezed past him he leaned in and tried to kiss me. I pushed him away but laughed, and told him I didn't even know his name. He was really drunk by then. And that was it. I left, and didn't think about him again.

A couple of weeks later I met up with Sacha and Ed, who told me that surfer guy was keen to catch up with me. I wasn't enthusiastic at first but, after Sacha's encouragement, I agreed that they could give him my phone number. A few days after that, I received a text message: *Hey sunshine, do you remember me? Would you like to catch up for a drink or dinner when you're in town again?* I was working hard and so didn't reply straightaway. About two weeks later Sacha asked me about it. She told me he was a nice guy and that I should give it a go.

So I did, and that's how I went to dinner with surfer guy and discovered his name was Ali Elamine and he was a couple of years older than me. He came straight from work, was dressed in a suit, had his hair slicked back, and was driving a brand-new flashy four-wheel drive with leather seats. It was such a change from the idiot goofball I'd met at the party that I reassessed what I thought of him. How shallow is that? All I can say is that back then I was young and still caught up in the dazzle. I suddenly thought that this man had some direction in life and was someone I could have an adult conversation with, and that was attractive. Anyway, it turned out to be quite a nice evening; I could have listened to that Californian accent for much longer. We ate at a Mexican restaurant that wasn't so flashy, but the food was good, and so, in a delightful surprise, was the company. At the end of the night I realised that I liked Ali.

We began to see each other every couple of weeks or so, when my flight schedule allowed. I was still a little wary;

my perception that he seemed keener than I was made me cautious. It was only when Ali became a little more reserved that I felt an urge to know him more, perhaps because it was like a chase, a bit of cat and mouse, and a need to know what made him tick. However, after a few months, I was bored with the whole game; I didn't seem to be getting to know him at all, so when I headed back to Brisbane for a four-week break at the end of the year I had little intention of keeping in touch. But there was something about Ali that I couldn't quite shake. I ended up sending him one text message, and he replied quickly.

Although I didn't miss him while I was home, there was still a part of me that wanted to contact Ali when I returned to Dubai. And that part won, because I rang him when I was disembarking. It was around 6am, so I didn't expect him to answer, but he picked up and we had a quick chat before he said he was heading out to surf. He promised to ring a bit later, but I didn't hear from him until late in the afternoon. Over the next few days Ali didn't seem in a hurry to catch up. *Fine*, I thought, *I can take a hint.* When we finally got together for a coffee, I told him I didn't think our relationship was working – if you could even call it a relationship – and I thought it was best if we went our separate ways. I was surprised by Ali's reaction: he seemed devastated, and pleaded with me to re-think what I was saying.

'I really do like you,' he said.

'That's not the vibe I get.'

Well, from that moment the vibe changed. Roses were soon left at my door, and in the following phone conversations, then get-togethers, Ali couldn't have been more charming. And, I have to admit, I began to fall for him. He was funny, engaging, and just good fun to be with. The more I fell for his personality, the more I was attracted to his looks, especially his eyes and smile. And as I'd already learned from a certain Dallas police officer, I was a sucker for the way American guys spoke. But Ali's accent came with some mysteries. He told me he'd grown up in Huntington Beach, California, with his grandmother. As for the rest of his family? I probed, but Ali didn't give much away. Eventually, he told me his family lived in Lebanon and travelled every now and then to the United States.

'Are they ever in Dubai?' I asked.

'Sometimes.'

'I'd love to meet them next time they're here.'

I assumed he would tell me more in his own good time, so I didn't press. Meanwhile, our relationship grew stronger. It's here I acknowledge that I was, not for the first time, relishing the Dubai lifestyle we were both living. Ali bought me expensive gifts and took me out to ritzy restaurants, where our bills would top hundreds of dollars. He didn't mind flashing his cash around; there were times we'd go out for drinks and he'd shout lots of people and run up huge bar tabs without a thought. He'd just slap down his credit card and say: 'I'll get it.' He was a manager for a property development company and he certainly knew the walk and talk. Even when we were relaxing at a beach he could pull off a deal over the phone. It was a funny sight, seeing him wheeling and dealing on the mobile while walking around barefoot in board shorts. And, yes, that all appealed to me at the time.

In December 2009, Ali and I flew to Australia for a holiday, and for him to meet my family. This was a very big deal for me. Family is everything, and their opinion of Ali mattered. Mum and Dad liked him straightaway. Simon was a bit cautious at first, but he was more comfortable as time passed, and Bryce was really enthusiastic because Ali, like Bryce, loved skating and scooters.

It was all going well, until the day Ali took one of many calls on his mobile. We were at Mum's place. Ali was outside, his back was to me and he didn't hear me open a door and walk out to join him. In the year or so I'd known him, I'd only ever heard him speak English, but suddenly I was listening to him speak Arabic. I was surprised – I didn't know he was fluent in another language, and it made me wonder what else I didn't know about him. When Ali finally saw me, he quickly hung up. I asked him why he'd never told me he spoke Arabic. We began to argue, and I became very confused. He said he didn't think Lebanese men were highly regarded in Dubai, so he'd downplayed his heritage. Downplayed was an understatement – he had played the part of a Californian surfer boy perfectly. I couldn't understand any of it; I had never judged someone by their heritage.

After I pushed him for answers he told me he'd been speaking with his brother.

'So, your brother speaks fluent Arabic too? It's obviously not something you've just learned.'

'No, the whole family speaks Arabic.'

Of course they did. Silly me. Was I making something out of nothing? I couldn't understand why Ali was trying to avoid his heritage. He was Lebanese. So what? Eventually Ali gave me some insight into his family – including the fact that his whole family lived in Dubai, just a short distance from my apartment. Apparently Ali's mother didn't want to meet me because, being Australian, I would only be in Ali's life for a short time; I wasn't someone she could see her son marrying. I was stunned and upset when he told me this. I tried to find out more, but with a lot of huff and puff Ali said: 'Just get over it.'

I was beginning to realise how little I knew about Ali, but at a stage when so many others in a similar position might have run, it just made me more determined to meet his family and find out more. And the truth was, I had already fallen for Ali, and as many of us know, love can tie us to torments that we either ignore or choose to do nothing about.

After that incident Ali continued to answer calls, but he never again attempted to hide his Arabic. I was glad, and I felt like we were growing closer. Things seemed good between us. I couldn't help but think about Ali's mother, though, and I hoped that one day we would meet and she would accept me.

After two weeks, Ali and I returned to Dubai and easily fitted back into the lifestyle. I was falling more in love with him, but it didn't seem to be going anywhere – perhaps because my job ensured we didn't see a lot of each other. By the end of the year we came to the crossroads. My three-year contract with Emirates was nearly up, and I'd decided I'd had enough of being a hostie and would return to Australia to look for other opportunities. I told Ali about my plans and wasn't surprised when he said he liked Australia but didn't want to move there. So, that was it. It was going to come to an end. It seemed to me it was time to call quits on our relationship and move on.

If only it could have been that simple.

Chapter Five

Despite knowing I was in love with Ali, I started to wind up my life in Dubai. I knew that it would hurt but I told myself I would get over him. Then, about two weeks before I was due to fly back to Australia I discovered I was pregnant. I was twenty-four years old. I was shocked. For as long as I could remember I'd wanted to be a mother one day, but from my late teens I had had a peculiar belief that I would never be able to have children. I don't know why; it was just one of those strange thoughts that would creep into my mind every now and again. It was probably tied into my Crohn's and the problems of living with a chronic disease. Ali and I had been lax about birth control, but I knew my cycle and thought I was safe. I was wrong. Although excited, I was also worried how Ali would react. I knew this would complicate things; being an unmarried, pregnant, Western woman in a Muslim country was not at all a pleasing thought. Ali was away working in Oman, and I rang to tell him the news.

'I'll come back straightaway,' he said.

'Why? You're coming home in a couple of days; that's soon enough.'

But Ali was adamant, and later that day he arrived at my apartment. He was distressed, and I couldn't blame him.

'We'll fix this problem,' he told me.

But to me, it wasn't a problem, and there was certainly no need to fix it. Being a mother was something I'd always wanted, so I tried to calm him down by saying that I wasn't worried, but that made it worse. I understood Ali might have felt scared; this was huge news to deal with. I assumed he was in shock and was worried about his future. I wasn't pressuring Ali nor was I trying to trap him, but I had pretty much decided I was having the baby. I couldn't imagine the alternative.

Over the following days I told some close friends and rang Mum and Dad to tell them the news, and they were all excited. But I still didn't know for sure what Ali was thinking until he point-blank told me that I should have an abortion. That upset me and I told him I wouldn't even discuss it, much less do it.

Things were tense when I departed for Brisbane in February 2010, well and truly ready to raise our child by myself. I had managed to save a bit of extra money, and in a matter of days after I got home I landed a job in human resources. When I added my family and friends to my support base, I was certain I had the means, both financial and otherwise, to make single motherhood work. At the time, I didn't realise how hard that could be, but even if I had I know I'd feel the same way. Most of all, I had the love and desire; I wanted nothing more than to be a mum.

What should have been a joyful time, however, turned into a stressful hell because Ali remained adamant that an abortion was my only option. He emailed, phoned and texted constantly. I felt he pushed and pushed me to give in. I knew this was all unplanned and a massive shock, but Ali appeared to give no thought to the way I felt. I told him I could never live with myself if I ended this pregnancy. I reassured him he didn't have to have anything to do with me or the baby and that I would make no financial demands – but I wouldn't give in to him. That didn't stop him.

Eventually, all the anger and bitterness he was experiencing boiled over one morning when I was in my apartment with my friend Dana, whom I had met when we both lived in Dubai. Dana had also returned full-time to Australia, and had become one of my closest friends. We were chatting away when the phone rang.

'Here we go,' I said to Dana when I saw that the caller was Ali. 'I'm about to get an earful.'

'Well, don't answer it.'

I wanted someone else to hear what I was going through so I could talk about it and get some advice, so I said, 'No. Just listen to what he says.'

I answered the call on speaker, and before I could say more than hello, Ali launched into a rant and asked me if I was going to have an abortion.

'You're fuckin' selfish!' he shouted. 'You're going to ruin both our lives.'

I could tell from Dana's expression that she couldn't believe what she'd heard. She leaned into the phone: 'Hi, Ali, this is Dana. Remember me?'

Hearing her voice made Ali angrier. He swore at me, and yelled that it was no one else's business. I burst into tears, and Dana took the phone off speaker and left the room with it. I don't know what she said to Ali, but a few minutes later she came back in and said, 'Don't have anything to do with him.'

'I have to. It's his child too.'

I only wish I'd had the courage to follow Dana's advice. Now, as I write this book, I think what would have happened if I'd lied. I know that would have denied our child a parent, something I don't think any person should do, but if I had told Ali I would do what he asked, then he would never have had a reason to see me again. I couldn't do that.

When I was about six months' pregnant I came home to my mum's apartment after having an ultrasound scan, and was bewildered by what I saw: there were rose petals scattered over the front doorstep, leading all the way along the hallway to the kitchen. I walked in and my jaw dropped. Ali was there.

'Oh my God, look at you,' he said.

'What are you doing here?'

Mum had apparently given him a key.

I stood there staring at him.

He took a blue ring box out of his pocket, got down on a bended knee and . . . My goodness, was this really happening?

'Will you marry me?'

'Um, I, um, I don't know.'

'It's just a "yes" or a "no".'

'Yes.'

He got up, and with shaking hands, he put a diamond-encrusted white-gold ring on my finger. Then he hugged me – he had never been overly affectionate – and asked if I was okay.

I don't think I really understood what we'd just done. It was bizarre: in an instant all his anger and doubt about having a child and all my confusion were erased. I made excuses to myself for his behaviour. All that mattered was that I was going to be a mum and Ali and I were going to be a family.

Mum was very supportive of our decision. She'd had her worries about Ali but believed he just needed time to deal with everything in his own way; she thought his proposal signalled a coming of age for him. Meanwhile, Dad was excited. He knew nothing of what led up to the proposal, and had only ever seen Ali at his charismatic best. Nearly all my friends were pleased too. Of course, Dana was wary after what she'd experienced, but others considered the news as a logical progression for Ali and me.

Ali stayed in Brisbane for a short time before returning to Dubai and things were good. He was attentive and loving. He planned to come out again well before the birth and wedding. He seemed comfortable with the knowledge he would soon be living in Australia for the foreseeable future and didn't suggest living elsewhere. Perhaps his position was made easier by the effects of the global financial crisis; he had lost his job in Dubai and was holding himself over by doing some property development work for his brother. The details he shared were sketchy even though we were in touch daily. And the mysteries continued when he fell out of contact for a few days. I had no idea what had happened, and, not surprisingly, the doubts didn't take long to surface. Was I suddenly on this journey alone after all?

Again it was a phone call that gave me some sort of answer – but this time it wasn't from Ali. One of his best friends back in Dubai, PJ, informed me that Ali was in jail.

Apparently he'd had some sort of traffic altercation. PJ said everything was under control and Ali would soon be released. My initial thought was: *Ali, you idiot!* About a week later, Ali rang me and apologised; I'd never been so grateful to hear from him. Apparently he'd been driving when someone cut him off on a side road. Ali beeped his horn and raised a rude finger, which the driver saw in his rear-view mirror. It just so happened that the driver was an off-duty police officer. So, it was off to a concrete cell until Ali's brother could arrange a lawyer and bail. Ali said the issue was now over. I believed him, but I was still worried: what else could go wrong? And in hindsight, I still ask myself: What on earth had I come to accept as normal?

Despite all the stress, I had an incredibly smooth pregnancy, which was made even easier by my mum. She created a ritual for us, in which we would attend each scan together and then go to buy a few baby things. She was in her element, especially when she started to make quilts and clothes. Her never-ending support drew me closer to her and made me appreciate even more the beautiful bond between mother and daughter; it was what I hoped to one day have.

Like the pregnancy, the birth was trouble-free. Our beautiful baby was born on 4 October 2010. I was in labour for about three hours, from start to finish. Admittedly, I thought I was going to die during that time, but considering what most mums go through, I was lucky. It was a water birth at the Royal Brisbane and Women's Hospital. The process was all very natural: candles, music, incense, no drugs. It might seem strange to say it, but with so much going on, and with my emotions all over the place, I overlooked one very basic thing. Here I was cradling this tiny, extraordinary being on my chest, counting its toes, checking its breathing, basking in the most exhilarating moment of my life, when my mum asked: 'Is it a boy or a girl?' The midwife made a hasty check.

'It's a boy,' she said. 'Sorry, no that's the umbilical cord. It's a girl.'

Ali, who had arrived a few weeks earlier, was in the bath with me. For the first time ever, I saw him cry. Not just cry, but weep.

'Thanks, Sal, I'm proud of you. You did really well. Wow, look at her. She's perfect.'

When he held Leila for the first time, Ali was smitten. I initially thought he was behaving a little oddly, but in truth, it was his pure joy. I'd never seen it before. Perhaps it's not an unusual reaction for a man – that is, he doesn't really think the whole episode is real until he holds the baby, whereas a woman has already had months to bond with her child, feeling it move inside her. Little Leila lay in Ali's arms for ages; I knew from that moment how much Ali loved her. And all the horrible things that had happened between us suddenly didn't seem as important as making our little girl feel safe and loved.

That night, I was exhausted but I couldn't sleep. I sat up in bed and watched Leila in her cot. She didn't move, didn't do anything, really. And all I could do was stare at her beautiful face and all that hair. She had a lot of hair. I just wanted to pick her up and cherish every single second. I kept thinking: *My God, you're amazing. I can't believe Ali and I created you.* I was very much in a state of disbelief; that strange feeling I'd had about never having children floated into my thoughts. But there was no need to worry about that anymore. And if I had even the slightest doubt that all this was happening, the first breastfeeding attempt told me how very real everything was. It was such a special moment; so raw and stripped back. I didn't know what to do, but everything I did do seemed so natural, so right. I was a mum, and no one could ever take that greatest of joys and honours away from me. At least I didn't think they could.

From the moment Leila was born, I knew my chief role in life was to be there to shelter her, guide her, teach her – to do everything I could to set her on her own path. And even when she was on her way, I would always be there for her, just like my mum had been – and continues to be – for me. Basically, I didn't realise how much love I had to give until Leila came along.

You might be confused to hear me call my daughter Leila. That is what she was initially called – and Ali and I had every intention of officially naming her that – until Ali received a call from his cousin, Derek, in the United States, a few days after the birth.

'Do you pronounce it Lay-la or Lay-ella,' he asked.

I immediately liked how Lay-ella sounded. Ali agreed, and after I asked our little one, I thought she reckoned it was pretty cool too. However, we didn't know how we should spell it. A good friend helped out and sent us about ten different versions of the name. And that's how we came to settle on Lahela.

Lahela was a chilled baby, content to sleep and feed. That was a blessing for me because Ali and I had another event to prepare for: ten days after the birth, we were married in the Department of Births, Deaths and Marriages in Brisbane. Initially, we had planned to be married before Lahela was born, but her slightly premature arrival changed our plans in a hurry. We both agreed that a civil marriage was appropriate. He told me he was a Shia Muslim, although I didn't think he was a devout follower – I had never seen him pray – and I swayed towards Christianity, although I wasn't a church-goer. It might sound odd, but we had never really discussed these differences before. Perhaps it was a minor clash of religions, but that wasn't in our thoughts so it didn't worry either of us at all.

Two days later we had a small reception in Mum's back-yard. I hadn't long turned twenty-five, and Ali was a month shy of twenty-seven. I have never liked being the centre of attention, and celebrations for the marriage were no different. My family and a few close friends attended, and Ali had a mate come up from the Gold Coast. It didn't surprise me that none of his family was there. It was a long way for them to travel, and I still hadn't met them. By then, I knew he had two older brothers, Wissam and Rida, who were both married. I had in fact spoken to Wissam when he rang to congratulate us after Lahela was born. He seemed nice. But I had never spoken to Ali's mother or father.

The ongoing mysteries about Ali's family unsettled me. I didn't understand why he hadn't introduced me to his mum and dad, even by phone. I got the impression that Ali didn't care if his family knew me or not, which bothered me. But with our new baby and wedding to keep me busy, I didn't dwell on it. I thought time would change things and eventually all would be okay. At the reception I found out I had more to worry about. Ali was cooking at the barbeque and chatting away with others when I went over to him and asked if he wanted me to make him a plate of food.

He shook his head, and said, 'I have to leave.'

'Sorry, what?'

'I have to leave for Lebanon.'

'What do you mean you're leaving for Lebanon? We've just got married. We've just had a baby. And why Lebanon?' It was the first time he had mentioned it.

My husband of just two days told me his family had moved to Lebanon, and his mother was sick in hospital; she had a serious eye problem, and he needed to be there. He had never told me any of this – we were married, surely we should talk about everything – but I wasn't going to stop Ali if his mother was ill. I would do the same if our situations were reversed. Like I said, family is important.

Ali flew out the next day. Almost immediately, chilled little Lahela turned into a devil child who started to wake up and scream dozens of times a night. I was up and down, doing everything I could to settle her but nothing worked. Mum was my saviour; she took time off work, and would look after Lahela for a couple of hours every morning while I tried to double the amount of sleep I'd had. It was relentless. By the weekends I was absolutely shattered, and Mum again came to the rescue by taking Lahela away and bringing her back to me only for feeding. I would just lie in bed and re-charge; it was the only way I was able to keep going.

Mum thought Lahela had reflux – I didn't even know what that was – so we took her to a paediatrician, who agreed there was a slight problem but it wasn't bad enough to medicate. Lahela continued to scream through the night, and I was sleep-deprived and unsure. I wanted nothing more than to comfort my baby and I felt so hopeless and inadequate; perhaps it was inevitable that I would finally crack at some point. It happened in the car park of a shopping centre.

Lahela began to cry, and that set me off. I turned to Mum and said: 'Take her.' Then I walked away. I didn't know where I was going; I just had to walk, and get away from my screaming baby. I felt so useless and unable to settle her, and that combined with exhaustion left me defeated. And I missed Ali and was sad and resentful that we weren't sharing these early days with our daughter together. I think that was the weakest moment as a mother I have ever had. Bless my mum; I'm so glad she was there. As many new mothers know, that overwhelming feeling of helplessness is terrifying and seems insurmountable. I was at my wits' end.

Later, I rang Ali and, crying hysterically, I shouted: 'I hate you! How could you leave me?' He tried to calm me down, promising he would return soon. Gradually I did calm down and over the next few days the feelings of depression and exhaustion passed.

Over the following weeks, Lahela settled. However, she still had her moments. For months she needed to be held to sleep. She was never one of those babies who could be put down and drift into dreamland by the time the nursery door was shut, nor was I a mother who adhered to controlled-crying practices. I wouldn't let her cry for more than a few moments before the overwhelming urge to pick her up took over and I'd hold her in my arms until she was asleep.

When Ali returned after about a fortnight I was so glad to have him back. I asked him about his family and his mother, but he tried to dismiss my questions about his mother's health – I had also asked him about her over the phone – and the only thing he said about her was: 'She's not well. She's in hospital.' So, with that part of his life still a mystery to me, we tried to work on building our own family life. I have to admit Ali tried really hard to share the load in looking after Lahela. I appreciated the effort he made, and I tried to understand that the whole baby thing was new to him as well, and we each had our own ways of working through it and learning from it. There is a saying that 'When a child is born, so is a parent.' How very true.

All went well between us for a few weeks, and I grew more comfortable with our relationship again, although I was still cautious. And soon enough, that feeling was justified.

On the day we were driving into Brisbane city to lodge paperwork for Ali's temporary resident visa, I had a strange feeling that he was keeping something from me. He just seemed to be holding back.

'Are you sure you want to do this?' I asked him.

'Yes, why?'

'I feel like the only reason you will live in Australia is because of Lahela.'

'No, that's not true.'

His answer wasn't very convincing, so I pushed him some more by telling him that I thought he only married me because of our child. I hoped that wasn't true and he'd reassure me.

'Am I right?' I asked.

He talked around the answer, and after I continued to push him, he suddenly pulled over to the side of the road.

'My brother rang me the other night. He asked if I wanted to work in Lebanon with him.'

I heard Ali out. His oldest brother, Wissam, who was always negotiating some type of business deal, was about to begin building and selling two blocks of apartments in a new area of Beirut. He proposed that Ali manage the project and potentially become an investor. Apparently there was quite a lot of money that could be earned in just twelve months. Although I was surprised by the news, I was willing to listen. The money could set us up very well, and with Ali having the security of guaranteed work, we could surely settle into some sort of family routine.

'What's Lebanon like?' I asked.

'I don't know. I've never lived there.'

'But your parents are from there.'

'Yeah, but I grew up in California, remember.'

I was still to get to the bottom of his childhood, but that was to be a discussion for another day.

As much as I questioned Ali, it was the questions that I had to ask myself that needed most attention. I knew nothing about Lebanon; I'd only ever been there on a turnaround flight to Beirut and had seen little more than a baggage handler's wave. I knew the country had been through war and political turmoil, but I accepted Ali's assurance – despite apparently never having lived there – that it was now safe. Perhaps it was worth a go? I was used to travelling, so that wouldn't be a problem for me. And Lahela was too young to know any different. Then, when she grew older and was back in Australia, I could tell her about her year in Lebanon, and she could have something different to talk about with her school friends. It could be quite an experience for us all. And life was all about experiences, wasn't it? At no stage while sitting in the car did I think at all logically. I didn't consider that I had no friends in Lebanon; that I would be a long way from my mum; and that I was a young mum with a baby. I didn't consider how tough it could be. Overall, I thought: Lebanon, money, a good foundation for our family, do it for Ali. And we could support each other and strengthen our relationship; it would just be us.

'All right, let's do it,' I told him there and then.

'Are you sure?'

Clearly he was surprised. But there was little further discussion. We were moving to Beirut.

I didn't know what the hell I was getting myself into.

Chapter Six

Saying goodbye to my mum was harder than I had imagined, but I was happy to be supporting Ali and so at the end of March 2011 we flew to Beirut. Lahela was almost six months old. Ali's parents met us at the airport and I finally got to meet them face to face. I was nervous – I knew that my mother-in-law, Ibtissam, didn't speak English, but she had a huge smile on her face and she hugged me as we greeted each other. It took me by surprise but made me feel welcome. Ali's father, Zeid, was more reserved, but not unfriendly. Ibtissam wore sunglasses and a headscarf, Zeid was dressed in a suit, and he shook my hand, kissed me on either cheek, and unlike his wife he spoke a few limited words of English. However, nothing much was understood until Ali stepped in to translate.

It was late afternoon, and the sun was setting quickly. I had that strange sense of disconnectedness that can come after a long flight. I most remember the dips in the road as we walked to the car park; there were lots of puddles, and by the time we reached the car the cuffs of my jeans were really wet. The other strong memory I have is of the brand-new Mercedes that Ibtissam – another surprise – drove.

I was too tired to observe much on our twenty-minute drive into the city. We stopped at an apartment block in a built-up area of shops, and took a lift to the sixth floor, the top floor. A maid opened the door to an apartment, and within minutes we were being fussed over by Ali's mum as she prepared a table full of humus, bread, tabouli, and a variety of traditional Lebanese foods. I was starving, so it was perfect. By then, it was quite cold, and Ali's mum pulled out some blankets, and gestured at me to get a second pair of socks for Lahela. I returned and started to put them on my daughter while she sat on her grandmother's lap – but I was suddenly stopped. Through hand signals and head shaking, Ali's mum left me in no doubt that I wasn't putting the socks on correctly. I didn't protest.

Soon afterwards, I put Lahela into a cot in Ali's and my bedroom. She and I both went to sleep quickly, while Ali stayed up late talking with his parents.

The next morning, I woke up feeling jet-lagged. I had a quick breakfast, and although I would have liked more rest, I couldn't say no to Ali's mum when she asked me to help her peel some beans in the kitchen. I wanted to make a good impression. As we worked, we tried our best to communicate by sign language, but we both became a little frustrated at our inability to understand each other properly. We continued to peel in silence until my fingers became too itchy from tiny hairs on the beans. I was being precious, but I tried to make a joke of it, telling Ali's mum of my irritation. She looked at me and said something in a tone that I could only interpret as sarcastic. Sometimes you don't need to understand the words. I tried to shrug it off but the welcoming feeling evaporated. I kept working for a while longer but then heard Lahela wake, so I went and got her and carried her back into the kitchen. Ali's mum wanted me to hand over Lahela to the family maid. I refused politely, and resumed peeling beans while Lahela sat on my lap. We didn't talk and I thought I sensed that Ali's mum was cross, but I put it down to my tiredness and jet-lag exaggerating my emotions.

Ali's parents stayed with us for a few days before they returned to their home in Chakra, a town about two hours' drive away. As much as I was looking forward to getting to know Ali's parents, I was relieved when they'd gone and it was just us. The quieter atmosphere gave me a chance to settle into our new home and spend time with Ali. The apartment had three bedrooms, a kitchen, bathroom, living area, and two balconies that looked out at other similar concrete buildings. Its most telling feature, though, was its white marble floor, which I soon found out would cause me great angst whenever Ali's mum came to visit. She would turn up regularly, and after taking her shoes off at the front door she would sit on the couch and then examine her socks to see how much dirt she had collected on the walk from the front door to her seat. If she wasn't satisfied with the cleanliness, she would tell her maid, who was always with her, to do a more thorough job. The first time it happened I felt humiliated. I didn't want it to happen again, so as a result I spent hours cleaning, sweeping and polishing to be ready for the next sock inspection; the pressure I felt was made worse by the generators on our rooftop – and all the other generators on other nearby rooftops – that left fine layers of black diesel dust everywhere. It was a constant battle to keep the floor clean and head off my mother-in-law's disapproval, and it didn't make me feel at all well liked.

The one Arabic word that sticks in my mind more than any other is *kahraba*: electricity. Power – or the lack of it – was the bane of my existence, and the dull lawn-mower-type whine of the generators became a familiar sound whenever our grid had enforced electricity outages. Ali told me there wasn't enough power to run the whole city at once, grids had rostered usage periods that were generally between three and six hours long. One day I returned home after buying groceries, including several heavy bottles of water, only to find the lift wasn't working because of a power shortage. I asked the apartment's maintenance man, '*Kahraba?*' But he shook his head. So, with Lahela in a sling across my chest, I managed to carry up all the supplies. No sooner had I reached the apartment than the *kahraba* came back on.

Gas came in bottles that Ali collected from a local store. At night, when the electricity was off and our generator didn't work, I became accustomed to bathing Lahela by torchlight in water that I warmed on a gas stove. It was very basic. I was often alone with Lahela at those times because Ali was out working, or doing something else; as was his way, he didn't tell me much about what he was doing. My wish for us to spend more time together and to rely on each other more wasn't really happening. Not for the first time, I hoped there would be a turning point and things would improve. I was bothered that he was away so often, but I was there to support him and this business venture so I tried not to let it get to me too much. I concentrated on Lahela and on making our home comfortable. I told myself that it wouldn't have been much different in Australia, if Ali was working hard I would have been home alone, but I was lying to myself because back there I would have had other support.

After a while the days just blended into each other with cleaning, looking after and playing with Lahela, and shopping for groceries, mostly at a fruit store only a hundred metres along the road. Occasionally I went further afield with Lahela and caught a taxi to the city centre to look around clothes shops such as H&M and Zara. Before getting into any taxi I always negotiated the fare with the driver to make sure I didn't get any nasty shocks when we reached our destination.

I was very careful, but about a month after we came to Beirut I had an experience that made me think about much more than haggling over Lebanese lirat. I'd just arrived outside the apartment block when I realised I didn't have the correct change. I apologised but that only made the driver angry. He started to shout right in my face. I shook as I held tightly onto Lahela.

Suddenly two guys, probably in their early twenties, came out from a nearby butcher's shop both carrying huge, long knives. A third man, a shopkeeper from across the street, appeared with a rifle. They all approached the driver and I assume they asked him what the problem was. In an instant all was settled. Lahela and I got out, and the driver sped off without accepting any money at all. The men asked me if I was okay. I was obviously shaken, so they took Lahela and me upstairs and saw that we made it safely into our apartment.

From what I could work out, the shopkeeper from across the street was a friend of Ali's. I didn't know it at the time, but we were living in a Hezbollah-controlled area. Was this what Ali had meant when he told me before we left Australia that Beirut was safe? I knew nothing about Hezbollah (Party of God) but was to learn it was a Shia political and military group that was immensely powerful throughout Lebanon. The party had risen during the early 1980s to fight against Israel when it occupied Lebanon, and had since grown to become one of the most influential forces in the country.

We were living on the outskirts of the suburb of Hadath near St Therese. The streets were full of hustle and bustle, and were often dirty and filled with rubbish. Everyone in the apartment block would put their garbage outside the front door where the block's maintenance man would pick it up and take it to a large industrial bin at the back. There, the rubbish pile would grow for about two weeks before a truck came along to lug it away. Despite this, the area could be pretty, especially at night when the lights of houses on the surrounding hills looked like stars reaching up to the sky.

There was also a vacant block of land nearby that had wavy grass tall enough to lose a small child in. Sometimes I'd look out over that block from the apartment and wish it could be turned into a children's playground; sadly there were no spaces nearby in which kids could run wild.

Every day I would wake up and learn something new about the suburb, Beirut or its people. One of the early lessons was about clothing. In public, I normally wore the same sort of clothes that I did in Brisbane: jeans and a

T-shirt or jumper. I was never asked to put on a headscarf, nor did I feel the need to. With green eyes and blonde hair I was always going to be noticed, and as time passed I accepted that I would cause a few sideways looks. I was used to that after my time in Dubai. But it was still easy to feel overwhelmed. It wasn't that I felt unsafe; it was more a case of constantly wondering if I was in too deep. Had I done the wrong thing? All I knew was that I had made a decision to live in Lebanon for twelve months to support Ali, and I was determined to do just that.

Obviously the strength of my will was likely to be influenced by Ali. As much as I learned about a country and culture that were so different from my own, my biggest lessons continued to be about my new husband. One day when driving in the family's BMW X5 I noticed a picture of a man on a roadside billboard. The face looked familiar – I had no idea why – and I mentioned it to Ali.

'You really don't know, do you?' he said.

'What do you mean?'

He told me the man was his mother's uncle who was a prominent politician. I didn't appreciate how powerful this association was until, on another occasion, Ali was pulled over by police for speeding on a freeway. The officer checked the registration and was immediately very apologetic. He allowed Ali to drive away without a ticket. Yet again I was left with more questions than answers: Who exactly was Ali? And his family? And me? Would I ever be let in?

Nearly every weekend we would go to stay with Ali's parents in Chakra. At first I was happy to do this because I wanted to get to know Ibtissam and Zeid and have them accept me and feel comfortable with me – and I wanted to do it away from the pressure of my white marble floor. The drive to the town didn't only open my eyes but showed how much I needed Ali for security and reassurance. At various times we would pass buildings pockmarked by bullets and mortars, or destroyed by bombs. Then there were the road checkpoints that were a collection of drums and sandbags, and rope-like devices with spikes that could be thrown out to puncture the tyres of any vehicles whose drivers didn't stop. The soldiers were always friendly with us. They would exchange greetings with Ali and we would be on our way again. It was my first experience of such military control anywhere in the world; if I hadn't been with Ali, I am pretty sure I would have gone crazy with fear.

Putting those experiences aside, I actually really enjoyed the drives. Until we reached Beirut's outskirts everything was quite grotty, but after we left the tired buildings and checkpoints behind, we headed into the hills, which were overlooked by snow-capped mountains. Ali always drove, while I stared out the window and cleared my mind. Although it was spring when we first arrived, the air was still cold, and the higher we went, the chillier and fresher it became. I felt cosy and content with the heater on, the seats warmed, and Lahela snugly wrapped up in her capsule in the back. I never felt more in love with Ali than when we took those drives. I needed him. And so did Lahela. We were all on this Lebanon adventure together, a young family trying to find its feet in the world.

Chakra was such a peaceful contrast to the noise of Beirut. Ali's parents lived in a large brick house with terracotta-like roof tiles and a marble floor. They were away from the heart of the town, and had a bigger block than many others nearby. *Kahraba* was a constant problem: lights would flicker on and off; the fridge would hum one minute and be dead quiet the next, and then we'd hear the whine of the generators and everything would start up again. In the centre of the town was a type of dam that, together with household tanks, provided the local water supply. Many of the roads were single-lane bitumen, and drivers always had to be very watchful, for both oncoming vehicles and the occasional man riding a horse.

My favourite place was just a few minutes' stroll up a hill from Ali's parents' home. I would take Lahela in a pram, passing a field of waving grain, and then stop at a small piece of land that looked towards the mountains. It was best to arrive in the late afternoon in time to watch the sunset: stunning red and gold streaks lit up the sky and painted clouds that I felt I could reach out and touch. If I turned my head one way, the wind would whistle into my ears; if I turned my head another way, there would be silence that was only broken by the occasional bird-call. I took many photos, and told Lahela how pretty it was. So tranquil.

Unfortunately, it wasn't as peaceful back in the home. Although I got on quite well with most of Ali's family – especially my sisters-in-law, Rema and Hora, and Ali's father, and brother Rida – I just couldn't build a balanced relationship with Ali's mum. At times she made me feel incredibly special, like when she served me first at dinner, which was considered a real honour. It would make me think we'd turned a corner and things were going to be better. But it wouldn't last and, generally, I sensed she had no real interest in getting to know me. By the time the weekends were over I was usually relieved to go back to the apartment to enjoy my own space. I would Skype my mum and vent my feelings about how difficult I was finding it to become part of my new family. Mum urged me to get along as best I could, and reminded me of the cultural differences between an older Lebanese woman and a young Australian. I don't think she realised how hard it really was. Her main worry was Ali.

'Are you still happy with him? Is he treating you well?'

'Yes, Mum.'

However, the closeness I'd felt on those drives to Chakra didn't last. One day I was doing my usual daily clean of the apartment when Ali rang me. He'd been out surfing and was on his way home.

'Do you want to go out for a bite to eat?' he asked.

'I'd love to, but I'm still cleaning.'

He didn't tell me to stop. Instead, he said he was going to pick up Wissam's wife, Rema, and her four children; we agreed that I would meet them all later. He then swung by the apartment, said a quick hello, picked up a couple of bottles of water, and left. I cleaned for another hour or more before I was sick of it. I called Ali. No answer. I tried again. Same result. I didn't want to be caged up in the apartment, so I decided to head downtown where I would try to ring Ali again. I caught a taxi with Lahela and we wandered around our usual haunt, H&M. I lost track of time and it wasn't until another hour had passed that I took my phone out of Lahela's nappy bag and noticed a few missed calls from Ali. I rang him straightaway.

'Where the hell are you?' he demanded.

I asked him why he was angry and explained that I had tried calling him earlier. That made no difference to him. The conversation went nowhere. I told Ali that Lahela and I had just sat down for a rest in a little French restaurant. He then hung up. Minutes later, he materialised out of nowhere and said angrily: 'Don't you ever do that again! Give me Lahela.'

'Why? What's wrong?'

He pulled Lahela off my lap, put her in the pram, ripped the nappy bag – which held my wallet and keys – from me and stormed off. It happened so quickly, and it left me stunned. I had no idea where he was going, or how I would get home.

I found a taxi driver and, with a combination of English and Arabic, was able to convince him that I would pay him once I could get into my apartment. We arrived home by early evening, but Ali wasn't there and I couldn't get in, so I ran back to the street and borrowed some money from a shopkeeper friend, Rami, and paid the taxi driver. I then returned to the building and sat on the fire escape in the darkness – the electricity was off – and waited. I was scared and tearful, frustrated and tired.

I don't know how much time passed before Ali walked up the stairs holding Lahela asleep on his shoulder.

'Where have you been, Ali?'

He brushed by me without saying a word, unlocked the apartment, went inside and slammed the door in my face.

'Ali, let me in.'

'No, get fucked!'

I sat down and bawled.

I was there maybe an hour, maybe much less; my mind wasn't in a fit state to know. I didn't understand what was happening.

The door finally opened and there was Ali. 'Are you all right?' he asked.

'Can you let me in?'

'Stop crying. The neighbours can hear. Get inside.'

I walked in. 'Why are you treating me like this?'

'Stop it. I don't want to hear your sob story. I've got work to do.'

Ali went and sat at his computer. I pleaded with him to listen to me, to talk with me.

'No, just go to bed. Get out of my face.'

'Please, why are you doing this? Don't you know I love you?'

Ali looked straight at me and said: 'Maybe you should act like it.'

That's when I lost it. I picked up my phone and hurled it at him. It just missed his head and it smashed against the door.

'That's great! You're not getting another one.'

'Talk to me!' I shouted.

I expected him to hit back with his own rage, but he did absolutely nothing. He just stared at me, emotionless.

I couldn't stand it. I picked up some books and threw them at him. I screamed at him, demanding that he talk to me. But he only told me to go to bed.

'You're annoying me,' he said.

I screamed again. Anything to get a reaction from him. It wasn't pretty and I am not proud of myself, but I was determined to talk it through and make sure it didn't happen again. This wasn't how I thought a loving husband should behave. I had done nothing wrong.

Suddenly Ali came towards me, and his expression frightened me. I turned away quickly, walked into our bedroom and slammed the door.

'Fine! Forget it!' I shouted more boldly than I felt, and hoped he wouldn't open the door.

That night, after I put Lahela to bed, I couldn't sleep. Ali made a bed on the couch in the living room. By the time I got up in the morning he was gone.

The tension lasted for two days, and then as if he could flick a switch, Ali was normal again. He was nice to me. I was so relieved, I decided not to drag the episode out. We'd had our argument. It was time to move on. I loved him. I wanted our marriage to work. He must have just been worried about Lahela and me, I told myself, it would never happen again.

Chapter Seven

Good days and bad – Ali and I had them both. Most of the time we got on well, and when we did we had our happiest moments. On those days, I never had any doubt that we had done the right thing by moving to Lebanon. However, to say the life there was still hard for me was as big an understatement as I could make. Even when Ali and I were getting along there were times I felt very lonely. Ali would often be out late – I assumed it was work, but I really had no idea what he was doing because he didn't tell me – and I would ring and ask where he was. He would say he was stuck in traffic or had just finished a long meeting or had seen some friends. He had many reasons, and I just had to accept them.

I also had to accept Beirut for what it was. If I had worried about all that could go wrong I would have taken Lahela back to Brisbane every second day. Whenever there were security fears the city tightened up in a heartbeat. One day Lahela and I were on our way back from shopping downtown when our taxi was stopped by soldiers and we all had to get out while the car was searched. It was standard procedure for every vehicle entering our neighbourhood. The reason? I think a bomb had gone off elsewhere in Beirut, or eighty kilometres north in Lebanon's second biggest city, Tripoli.

Another day, Lahela, Ali and I were walking to our car and just down the street police officers started shooting at two men on a motor scooter. The two men were shot in the legs.

As the police started firing Ali yelled at me to take cover. I was carrying Lahela and I ran behind a car and ducked down. It was all over very quickly, but the fact this happened so close to our home terrified me. Ali tried to reassure me and luckily Lahela was too young to understand what was happening. She didn't even cry.

After that, I told Ali I didn't feel safe but he convinced me it was all okay. Maybe I was in denial, but for me life continued as normal despite these tensions. Whatever normal actually was.

Throughout everything – good and bad – Lahela was my constant. She was so affectionate and cuddly, and looked at me with those big brown eyes in a way that I could never describe. I had a gut feeling that she was an old soul right from the moment she was born, and for as long as we were together we would look after each other. How was I to know how painful that feeling would turn out to be?

Lahela was about ten or so months old when we were in Chakra for one of our regular weekend visits to Ali's parents. Ali had travelled up with us but had since gone off somewhere without telling me where. It was just standard routine by then; I was always left with Lahela, and couldn't expect any help from Ali when it came to bathing, changing nappies, or any of the other must-dos that for parents quickly turn into thankless chores. I just accepted this was how it was. Despite growing up in America, it seemed that now we were living in Beirut, Ali was more influenced by traditional gender roles, and he now considered parenting to be a woman's work. I didn't mind that. Mothering Lahela was what I wanted to do, though it would have been nice to share some of those more thankless chores sometimes. I also wondered if Ali didn't want to be seen doing such things in front of his family.

While Ali was away I found that the family maid, who spoke reasonable English, was the only person with whom I could hold a conversation. On this particular day she came out of the kitchen holding a glass of water that she was going to take to a painter who was working in the house. I offered to take it for her. No problems. The painter was up a ladder and accepted the water with somewhat of a surprised look.

'*Shukraan* [thank you],' he said.

I went back to the kitchen, where I began to feed some pureed food to Lahela. Ali came back and said there were some friends I should meet. I followed him out to a covered patio where fifteen or so people, including Ali's brother, Wissam, had gathered. They were extended family. I was introduced to a maze of names and faces, and then I told Ali I wanted to take Lahela for a walk up to my favourite spot.

Not long after I began to push the pram up the hill, a car sped around the corner near me and its brakes slammed on. I looked over and saw that the driver was the house painter. He said something to me in Arabic that I didn't understand. To this day, I still don't know what he said. But I do remember his next words: 'Beautiful, beautiful.' I felt a little panicky because I didn't know what he was going to do. I turned and started to walk down the hill. The next minute, Ali and Wissam came flying up the road in the X5. The painter saw them and sped off. Ali pulled alongside me, wound down the window and asked angrily: 'What was that all about?'

I explained what had happened, including the 'beautiful' reference. Wissam was furious, seemingly a lot angrier than Ali.

Ali told me to go to the house. The painter arrived back not long after I did, and as he was getting some equipment out of his car, Ali pulled up and rushed over to him.

I watched in disbelief as my husband grabbed the painter by the shirt and shouted at him. It was ugly. Although I couldn't work out all that was being said, I knew what the message was: *Stay away from my wife.* The painter held his ground and spoke rapidly to Ali. Ali turned to me. 'He says you've been flirting with him. Have you?'

'I only gave him a glass of water.'

I laughed because it was so absurd.

'It's not funny!' shouted Ali.

All this was happening in front of the family to whom I had just been introduced. I felt embarrassed and didn't know where to look. Wissam wanted to take the matter further but was persuaded not to by his mother. She was, in fact, very protective of the painter because two years earlier he'd helped the family after Ali's father had suffered a stroke.

I thought it best to keep a low profile, so I took Lahela into our bedroom. But there was no chance of peace and quiet. Ali stormed in and accused me of leading on the painter. We argued fiercely. I was used to being the one who always backed down, but no, not this time.

I grabbed my passport – Lahela was included in mine – and I demanded: 'Take me back to Beirut; I want to go back to Australia. I'm not putting up with this.'

'You can go if you want, but you won't be taking Lahela.' He was cold, emotionless, but steely voiced.

'Well, I'm not going anywhere.'

Two weeks later we were still in Chakra. Ali didn't say one word to me during that time. And he didn't go to work either. However, he did go out for hours on end. I had no idea where or why. When he came back, I tried to reason with him, but he would look straight through me and walk past. Was it just a game to him? Or was it more serious than that – was he trying to show that he was in control? By then I realised that my ignorance of Lebanese culture had played a role in the whole miserable episode, but how was I to know what I should do in every single situation if no one helped me comprehend? It wasn't as though I had someone who was willing to guide me through my misunderstandings and mistakes. I was on my own. No close family. No friends. No one to turn to. Except beautiful Lahela.

At the end of that fortnight, I was woken by the sound of a car driving away from the house. It was 3am, and Ali was leaving. When he returned several hours later, he finally broke his silence. He said he'd been surfing. I knew the waves were his escape, a type of meditation for him, and I could only hope they had soothed him enough for us to speak sensibly about what had been happening. But, no, I was hoping for too much. He flatly questioned my judgment but wouldn't be drawn into a deeper discussion. Instead, showing no emotion at all, he said we were going back to Beirut.

I packed up everything and waited with Lahela. Was I glad we were going? Yes. But I was also worried about what might happen when we reached the other end. Ali was just so closed off, I didn't know how we could get past this.

By the time Ali decided it was time to leave, it was about midday. I said goodbye to his parents out by the car.

'Give Lahela to Mum,' said Ali. 'She wants to give her a cuddle.'

I did.

Then Ali's mum turned around with Lahela and walked back into the house.

'What's going on?' I asked.

'You're going back to Beirut.'

'Yeah, but where is your mum taking Lahela?'

'She's staying here, Sal.'

I could feel myself start to shake.

'Ali, I'm still breastfeeding. We can't leave our baby.'

'Lahela is staying here. And we are going to Beirut.'

I didn't move, which meant Ali had to push me into the car. I tried to get out, but Ali stopped me. I burst into tears as he started the car.

'Ali, please! Lahela doesn't have you or me. And your mum wouldn't know half her routine.'

'She'll be fine.'

I kept asking questions, but Ali didn't answer. He just drove away.

And I cried all the way back to Beirut.

By the time we were in our apartment I felt completely empty. My eyes hurt. My head ached.

'Please, Ali, tell me what is happening.'

'You're going back to Australia.'

'With Lahela?'

'No.'

One of the most vivid memories of my childhood is the day my nanna passed away. I'd never seen my mum more upset; she had a crazy, hysterical cry. Now, sitting in that Beirut apartment, I sounded just like my mum sounded that day.

Ali didn't say much. At that moment I hated him. And his mother too. My mind raced. How could they do this? Ali had ripped my daughter away from me and his mother appeared to be helping him. Lahela was my world.

That was only the beginning of my pain.

Ali took my passport and sim card, and ripped the Internet cable out of the modem and stomped on the plug. Then he told me he was going back to Chakra, and left me with only $100.

He came back two weeks later.

By then, I was broken.

Chapter Eight

I wouldn't wish anyone to go through the pain I did during those two weeks in the apartment without Lahela. I slept fitfully, barely ate, and spent most of the little money I had on bottled water because I'd been told if I drank out of the tap I would get sick. I also managed to buy a sim card but the directions were in Arabic, so I couldn't get my phone to work no matter how hard I tried; I randomly keyed in options, all without success. I didn't know who I could turn to. I didn't feel I could ask any of the shopkeepers to help me; they were Ali's friends and I was worried he would find out. I couldn't contact home and I didn't even think to try to get to the Australian embassy. I didn't want to do anything to antagonise Ali any further. I told myself I just had to wait until he calmed down and brought Lahela back to me.

I tormented myself endlessly with questions. Why was Ali doing this? What had I done wrong? How could his mother walk away with Lahela? The questions went around and around in my mind. Should I have agreed to live in Beirut with Lahela? Should I have tried to take her back to Australia after I first saw worrying signs? The answer to the last question troubled me most: I doubted Ali would have let me go. All I could do was wait. And hope. For the first few days I was in such denial that I expected Ali to walk through the door with Lahela at any moment, behaving as though nothing out of the ordinary had happened. But as the days passed, there was no news. And I was tearing apart. What was Ali doing? What was his mother doing? And poor Lahela?

After a week, I lost any sense of fight. I think now, I fell into a deep depression. I ached for my daughter. I was ashamed and I kept trying to downplay what Ali had done in my head because the horror that my husband could be so cruel was unbearable. I couldn't think straight. I wanted to contact my mum or my brothers but there was no way I could. I felt so far away and so helpless. I considered trying to get to Chakra, but even if I could have, I feared I would only anger Ali more. By now he had demonstrated to me he needed to be in control, so if I had arrived unannounced, God only knows what he might have done. Even writing those words make me shudder considering the decisions I would make later. All I could do was wait. I never went too far from the apartment in case Ali and Lahela returned. But this also tormented me. And trapped me. What would happen if Ali came back and he didn't want me to be there? Or would he have a worse reaction if I wasn't there? Already in this book I have spoken about not knowing many things about Ali. And I say it again now. It's all I can say. I didn't know what would happen. *I just did not know.*

Then Ali turned up.

'Where's Lahela?' I asked.

He chucked my passport at me.

'You're leaving tomorrow,' he said.

'Where to?'

'Australia.'

'But what about Lahela?'

I already knew the answer.

Chapter Nine

I was defeated. I didn't know how to argue, how to fight. The need to be with my daughter made my whole body ache, but Ali showed no sign that he cared. I didn't know what to do, so I did what Ali wanted. My only hope was that Ali would come around and soon change his mind. Before I left for Australia, he gave me his phone to ring my parents. I called Dad first; whenever there was some sort of family mishap – like a car accident – I always initially turned to Dad. I told him I was heading home, but didn't reveal Lahela was staying behind. Nevertheless, he sensed something was wrong. I texted Mum and she rang me on Ali's phone. She too realised not all was as it should be. However, it wasn't until I arrived in Brisbane at the end of August 2011 that my parents' fears were realised. They both came to the airport to pick me up, and Mum broke down as soon as she saw me walk out by myself.

I was still in denial, but Mum left me in no doubt about the seriousness of the situation. She was distraught and very, very angry. It was only then, in the company of the one person to whom I could tell everything, that I realised I might never see Lahela again. My baby was only eleven months old. I felt physically ill.

I'd lost several kilograms since I'd last seen Lahela and I only got thinner as I struggled every day and night with the position that I was in. I stayed at my mum's house, and my first priority was to seek legal advice. As a result, I applied through the Family Law Court for an order that prevented anyone other than me from taking Lahela outside Australia. That was a win of sorts. But what did it mean when my daughter was half a world away? I contemplated my options and found out for the first time about the Hague Convention, the multi-lateral treaty that enabled children to be expedited to their home country after being abducted to another. Did this apply to my situation? I put it on a list of things to find out. However, my main tactic remained hope; no matter how faint it may have seemed, I had to believe that everything would work out.

I rang or Skype-called Ali every day and pleaded with him to let Lahela come back. More often than not our conversations ended in arguments, and Ali would never let me talk with our daughter, or even see her. Then, he shocked me: 'I want a divorce.'

My heart broke during that call, and in the following ones he repeated his request time and again. After one of those calls, I walked out of Mum's house and headed down the driveway to meet Simon, who had just arrived with a friend.

'Jesus, are you all right? You look like shit,' he said.

I buckled over and fell to the ground. For whatever reason, Simon's comment sparked the moment that, I suppose, was always going to happen. I felt as though I was in hundreds of pieces on the driveway. I cried and trembled and felt so hopeless. Simon apologised – of course he didn't need to – and his friend quietly went back to his car. My brother helped me inside to my bed. I was so weak I could barely stand. Poor Simon; I don't think he knew how to deal with me and the whole situation. He wasn't married and didn't have children. It was so unfamiliar for him. He called Mum, who had just finished work. She was already fragile enough, and didn't need to see me like that. But when she did, we cried together. It was a rough afternoon, one that hit me hard. I felt I was losing my grip on Lahela, my life and my marriage. If I ever really had any grip at all.

And yet – and this is something I can't quite understand, so I am sure many readers will struggle with it as well – I still loved Ali. I so desperately wanted our marriage to work. I had seen my parents go through a divorce, and I didn't want that to happen to me. After watching Mum and Dad break apart I vowed to myself that I would work as hard as I could to repair any problems during my marriage. I didn't want peas on a floor to be an image that *my* children would remember. That might sound crazy, but it's the way I felt; to this day the memory of Dad walking out on Mum is a strong one for me. I was certainly influenced by my grandparents too. My grandma, who is ninety, still wears her wedding ring and talks about Grandpa as though he were still alive. For as long as I can remember, I have always craved what my grandparents had. And I still do.

Unfortunately, anything I said or pleaded seemed to mean nothing to Ali. He stared at me through the Skype screen with a cold and empty look that I had come to know all too well. It chilled me, but I couldn't give up. It seemed to me that the more emotion I poured into our discussions, the more Ali shut off. This was one of the most frustrating differences between us. I always believed conflicts were best handled by talking and looking for solutions, but Ali was the opposite: he locked himself up and let nothing out. The only breakthroughs I ever had were the rare times when Ali sent me photographs of Lahela via WhatsApp. I was grateful. She was growing without me but at least I could see her face.

But social media wasn't helpful when it was Ali who was looking at posted photographs. My closest friends knew what was happening and they were all wonderful, trying to keep my spirits buoyed. In a bid to cheer me up, some of them came around to Mum's house one evening and insisted I go out with them. I had been digging myself further into a hole, and they all wanted to try to make me smile for at least a couple of hours. The night was good fun – bless my friends – but after one of them took a picture and innocently posted it on Facebook it didn't take long for Ali to ring me. It was 3am, and he immediately launched into a tirade during which he accused me of being a horrible mother who didn't care that I wasn't with my baby. He couldn't believe I could actually go out 'partying', and he questioned if I was becoming a drunk. I replied with no emotion: 'Ali, I have nothing left to give to you. You've taken everything that I have.'

I was just so flat. Ali was winning.

I can't recall the exact timing, but he verbally abused me in a similar way when my hostie friend, Rachel, suggested I escape Brisbane for a few days and visit her mum, Kim, in Canberra. I was reluctant, but I couldn't refuse Rachel; she and other friends had been so kind to me. And the truth was, Lahela wasn't here, so there was no reason not to go. So, off I went, and one afternoon I agreed to go for after-work drinks with Kim. Of all the things that could have gone wrong, I would never have thought I'd end up sitting on a toilet floor of a bar, feeling dizzy and unable to move my hands. After Kim found me I was taken by ambulance and admitted to hospital. Blood tests revealed I'd had my drink spiked. I didn't know how it could have happened. I thought I'd been holding onto my glass of wine quite safely, but I must have turned my back or put it down at some stage. It was a terrifying experience and I was lucky it didn't turn out much worse.

Because of my time in hospital I didn't speak to Ali for a couple of days. When we finally did Skype again, I told him what had happened.

'It serves you right for drinking,' he said.

Nothing was more heartbreaking and hurtful, though, than what happened on 4 October, just over a month after I left Lebanon. It was Lahela's first birthday. If the pain of knowing that I couldn't be with her wasn't horrible enough, the actions of Ali ensured I would only ever remember the day with bitterness. He sent me a photo of Lahela being held by our sister-in-law, Rema, while his mother blew out the candles on a cake. A baby's first birthday. A milestone. And I wasn't there for Lahela. Her mother wasn't there. What else can I say? I couldn't see how things were going to change and I didn't know what else I could do. I had to steel myself and fight, find a lawyer in Lebanon to try to bring Lahela home, because by this point I didn't think Ali was going to change his mind.

It's impossible to know what life will throw at you. When you think that there is neither hope nor light, often something happens out of the blue. At around the time of Lahela's birthday, I was at a football-club fundraiser – despite not being very social, I was trying to keep myself busy – and I met someone I hadn't seen since we had both attended Albany Creek High. How different he was from the day he flashed by me on his way to start a fight. Brendan Pierce. He'd grown out of his wild teenage years to become an electrician. We had a quick chat that night, and he was kind and listened.

As time went on and Ali didn't come back with Lahela, Brendan and I caught up at other local get-togethers. He was very down to earth and I enjoyed his company. At that stage it was probably because he rekindled memories of school – happy, worry-free times. For some inexplicable reason I felt comfortable spilling all my problems to him. He said he was happy to listen, and true to his word he never got sick of listening to me or seeing me cry. He really felt for what I was going through. In a way, he became like a therapist. I hadn't sought any professional psychological help, but to have Brendan to turn to was perhaps even better. I began to appreciate our growing friendship, which was such a pleasant change from the party-party-can-I-have-your number-days of Dubai or the hot-and-cold intensity of Ali. I still hadn't given up on my marriage and I made that clear to Brendan, but I yearned for a simpler existence. Brendan, and so many other friends, helped provide that.

They also gave me some stability in my day-to-day life, which had become ruled by the unpredictable.

As I said, it's impossible to know what life will throw at you. Judging by the way my life had gone since I'd met Ali, I should have known there would be more surprises to come. Three months after Ali banished me from Lebanon, he rang me to say that he'd made a mistake and he wanted to work things out between us. He no longer wanted a divorce. He was coming to Australia – and he was bringing Lahela. It was like an electric shock. I couldn't believe my little girl was coming home. It was so unexpected that I found it almost impossible to believe him. What had caused the sudden turnaround? I thought back to an argument we'd had only a few days earlier. I'd told him I was so messed up that I just didn't care anymore.

'What else do you want from me, Ali? What else do you want?'

I hadn't shouted; I didn't have the energy.

I believe my flatness affected Ali. Was it possible that he was more positive towards me when I switched off and didn't react aggressively or tearfully? That question still plays on my mind today. He could always make me blame myself.

Chapter Ten

Lahela was coming home. I'd thought it would be a joyful moment, but it was devastating. Lahela didn't recognise me, and nor did she want to be held by me. She'd just arrived at Brisbane airport via Sydney, and even now I can't begin to imagine what she made of this strange lady in front of her who burst into tears as soon as she saw her. She didn't seem to know me at all and she had changed so much. She no longer had chubby cheeks, and her once curly hair was much straighter. She was thinner and taller too. But the most distinct change was in her eyes: they had a sadness that I had never seen before, a wariness that broke my heart.

All I wanted to do was hold her and tell her, 'Mummy is so happy to see you.' But she wouldn't leave Ali's side. Ali tried to coax her: 'Go with Mummy, go with Mummy.' But she wouldn't do it. From that day on, I never felt the same way about Ali, because he had broken the most important bond in life: the one between a mother and her child.

Over the next few days Ali worked desperately hard to repair the damage he'd caused; I realise now he had to, because Lahela was the last string of attachment between him and me. If Lahela didn't accept me, any chance of working on our marriage was over. As it was, I was still to decide if Ali was being genuine in what he was doing. I didn't know if I could ever trust him again.

It was a period of immense emotional overload. While Lahela went through a stage of working out who I was, Ali apologised to me for the mistakes he'd made. In response, I showed him the court order I'd been granted, and demanded he sign it if he truly wanted me to remain in his life. It was as heartless as I had ever been towards him. I didn't care if it turned him away or even if it led to divorce. He had pushed me too far.

The court order upset Ali. Again, I didn't care. I wanted him to see how angry I was. How dare he mess with our daughter's life and try to destroy mine? His heartlessness had consequences, which even he could plainly see in the way Lahela acted towards me.

He signed the document within a few hours and then did something I didn't expect: he bawled his eyes out. He promised that he would change and would never keep our daughter from me again.

'I want us all to be a family,' he said.

He stressed he would do anything to keep us together. And if that meant him going back to Lebanon for a while without us, so be it. For several days more, he told me the same sorts of things time and again. He told me everything I needed to hear and gradually he started to win me over. He even assured me that he would distance me from his mother. I wasn't completely convinced. Ali accepted that I needed time to think about everything; he didn't pressure me into making any quick decisions. It couldn't have been easy for him because up until then he was used to controlling the situation. Perhaps I made it worse when, after Ali had stayed at my mum's place for a couple of days, I asked him to find somewhere else to stay. However, he still visited every day.

By then, Lahela was no longer uncertain about me, though she still veered towards Ali most of the time. Unexpectedly, it was a reaction from Ali that finally led to a breakthrough moment in re-establishing my relationship with my daughter. During another tense discussion in which Ali told me he didn't deserve me, he broke down in tears, and no sooner had he started to cry than Lahela hugged me tightly and wouldn't let go. That in turn made me cry, and all I could think was: *This is all just so screwed up!*

Ali headed back to Lebanon after a few weeks. Neither of us knew what would happen between us but I was still that woman who wanted her marriage to work. It was all up to me.

While still weighing up my options, I held a belated first birthday party for Lahela at Mum's place. Family and friends came, and amid the celebrations there was plenty of quiet advice given to me, most of which could be summed up in three words: *Don't go back.* If roles were reversed and I was a friend looking at someone in my shoes, I would have said something stronger: *You're an idiot if you go back.* But it was never going to be as simple as that. The fact that I didn't feel as close to Ali as I once did was itself a problem, because, in my exhausted mind, I thought the only person who could put me back together was the person who had taken me apart. Weird, I know. Love can do that to you. It warps your thoughts and can trap you in the memories of good times, even though it's the bad times that you really should pay attention to. And when those warped thoughts and memories are added to the strongest of desires to give everything you have to make a marriage work, there is the chance that you have created a recipe for disaster.

Against the advice of everyone, I returned to Beirut in January 2012. It had been three months since Lahela had been brought back to me. During that time Ali and I were in contact pretty well every day, mostly by Skype. The more I switched off, the more he stepped up emotionally, telling me again and again that he was sorry. It got to me, and seemed louder than everything my family and friends had been telling me. It drowned out the despair I'd felt and blocked out the emotions I'd had when Lahela wasn't with me. Now she was back in my arms I didn't want to revisit those feelings – they were too painful. The memories of the good times between us grew stronger, and so did the thoughts of what I was doing to Lahela: I was keeping her from her daddy, and that wasn't fair on either her or Ali.

When I told Mum my decision, she walked out of the room in tears. I felt horrible. I also lost some friends. The hurt was very real for all of us, but no one could truly understand. How could they? Because they weren't me. And if at the time I had assessed my own character, there was one weakness that was more powerful than all my other weaknesses and strengths put together. It was Ali himself.

Chapter Eleven

Back in Beirut, things did change. Most of all, Ali kept to his promise that I would have little direct contact with his mother. I did not see her at all for the first three months after Lahela and I returned. That made me feel much more comfortable. I had less company, but also less stress. Ali and I worked on becoming our own little family with Lahela, who was at the stage of sounding out a few words. How wonderful it was to hear 'Mum-um'. I lifted every time I heard it.

Ali was also happy. Although his property development project hadn't worked out as well as he'd hoped, he was excited about a new venture that we both knew he would put his heart and soul into: he was going to set up a surf school. Of all the jobs he'd had, there would never be a better fit for him than having waves as his office. He was really busy building the foundations, and was away from our apartment for long hours. He had so much to do: advertising strategies, meeting and building relationships with the owners of sports stores, ordering boards and wetsuits, and when time allowed, conducting the occasional lesson or getting out for a surf himself. If all went well, he planned to officially open for business by the end of the year. He was excited and happy and he shared his plans and thoughts with me, which was all I'd ever wanted – to be a partnership.

Our relationship strengthened, and for the first time in a long time I was hopeful that we would only get stronger together as a couple and a family. I was starting to trust him again. The marriage was going to work. I knew it could. We started to talk about the future, and we both agreed that we would like more children. So, we started to try, and by the end of February I was pregnant – and thrilled.

When I told Ali, however, he looked shocked.

'Are you happy?' I asked.

'I don't know, Sal.'

At least he was honest, I told myself.

He left for work. It was early in the morning. I knew I didn't love him as much as I could, and deep down I still felt resentment towards him, but all the signs since I'd returned to Beirut were so positive that I felt Ali would jump at the news of the pregnancy. How wrong I was, and I was left wondering what the hell was wrong with him.

That evening he came back with a bunch of flowers and an apology. He said he was overwhelmed because the conception had happened so quickly. I accepted that, and over the following months I gave it no thought because Ali treated me really well. It was like he was wooing me all over again. Dinners, gifts, more flowers. Furthermore, he still kept me away from his mother, and the only contact we had was over the phone. She was excited when we told her I was pregnant. Considering our history, I thought her reaction was a little odd, but then I hoped she had also moved on from our earlier problems. So, all was smooth enough between us, and when we finally did see each other in Chakra, there were no signs I should be worried.

However, just when I thought things were finally okay, Ali and I went into another rocky patch. I don't know how it started. It just happened. For whatever reason Ali turned back to his cold, emotionless side, and as a result, I switched off too. One of our most troubling issues became where the baby would be born. Ali was keen to use a local hospital, but I was adamant I would return to Australia where I was more comfortable with facilities and had my family and broader support base. Our disagreements were often heated. Finally, I agreed we would at least explore the hospital possibilities in Beirut, but when Ali discovered how expensive it would be to use a top-class facility, especially if I was to need emergency procedures such as a Caesarean or an epidural, he reconsidered his view. My mum also played on his thoughts. On one particular Skype-call, she became very emotional and agitated – hysterical, you could say – and begged Ali to let me return home. Ali gave in, and I planned – with relief – to return to the Royal Brisbane and Women's Hospital.

As was the case when I carried Lahela, my pregnancy was trouble free. Ali and I found out early in the piece that we were going to have a boy, and we'd already decided on the name Noah because it was one that Ali had liked since his teenage years. In the final months I couldn't wait to be back on home soil.

In the meantime, my days in Lebanon fell into a routine I knew well: cleaning, looking after Lahela and shopping. Occasionally, we headed to Chakra. Each trip there made me more anxious, because tensions seemed to me to be rising again, and when I was about seven months pregnant my mother-in-law and I had an altercation that shocked me. It happened in the kitchen, where I was cutting up food with Ali's mum and my sister-in-law, Rema. They were speaking in Arabic, and although I had been working on my Arabic and could understand a little more, I couldn't follow much of the conversation. When I spoke with Rema I used English, which infuriated Ali's mother. It was a barrier and it amplified everything. I didn't realise how much of a problem it was until Ali's mum told me I was very rude and demanded I speak Arabic. She was chopping ingredients for a meal and had a knife in her hand. I am not proud that I laughed at her, but at first I thought she was joking. She looked at me and came towards me, raging. It freaked me out.

'What are you doing?' I said loudly.

Rema started to speak very intensely to Ali's mum, and persuaded her to step away. I was shaking, Rema was obviously shocked, and Ali's mum shouted at me to leave. I threw all the food I was holding onto a bench, and walked out.

Ali wasn't home at the time. When he returned he found me in our bedroom with Lahela, who had slept through the whole ordeal. Ali could see I'd been crying.

'Sal, are you all right?' he asked.

'No, I am *not*. Your mother is crazy.'

'Don't say that.'

I told him what had happened and then said some terrible things about Ibtissam, which not surprisingly fired up a huge argument. Ali leaped to his mother's defence, but I was in no mood to back down.

Finally he simply said: 'Leave it to me.' Then he walked out and shut the door behind me. I stayed in the room with Lahela for the rest of the evening. I was back to a very familiar place, wondering what on earth was going to happen next.

We left Chakra quickly and I made sure Lahela was never out of my sight until we were in the car driving away. Back in the apartment, things remained tense all the way up to

Lahela's and my departure for Brisbane not long before my twenty-seventh birthday at the end of September. In a reversal of fortunes, it meant that Ali wouldn't be present for Lahela's second birthday on 4 October. I knew what that felt like, so I held off celebrating it until Ali arrived to be with me for Noah's birth.

Our little man came along on 3 November. He was a lot fairer than baby Lahela had been, and had the broad-shouldered body of Ali. There were no complications. Again, Ali was genuinely emotional and teary, and I found myself looking at his reaction as much as I stared down at Noah. Ali stayed for a couple of weeks before flying back to Beirut, and leaving me with my mum to look after a baby and a toddler. I'd always been close to my mother, but our bond grew even tighter after I had my own children to look after. In those early days with Noah, Mum always anticipated what needed to be done; I guess that came from going through the process three times herself, but I never really appreciated what that truly meant until I was the one on call 24/7. Being a parent is the greatest responsibility that a human being can ever know. And it's only once you become one that you begin to realise how much your parents did for you, and how much you owe them.

Noah's arrival also confirmed to me that Lahela was definitely an old soul. Her sense of caring for her little brother was apparent right from the start. She'd stroke his head and hold his hands so gently. When you have children you rarely want to wish away time, but I must admit I couldn't wait to see them play together and look after each other when they were older.

Ali and I hadn't made a firm decision about when I would take the children back to Lebanon, but when Noah was nearly five months old I felt the time was as good as any. I didn't want to leave, but the same old reason pushed me: I had a marriage to fight for. Ali and I had continued to have our ups and down via Skype, and I hoped that my return with the children would settle things down between us and reinforce to Ali that I wasn't going to give up.

At the time of my arrival with the children at the end of March 2013, Lebanon was never far away from being mentioned on international news services because of its proximity to Syria; they were neighbours, and with Syria torn by civil war for more than two years, it was inevitable that Lebanon would be affected in various ways. However, Ali downplayed any reports that Lebanon wasn't a safe place to be. I accepted that, but also realised that the Lebanese people were used to walking on eggshells, and their interpretation of a normal daily life wasn't the same as someone's from a country that didn't have a history of conflict both inside its own borders and on its doorstep. Should I have been more concerned? Perhaps. But I was a mum to two young children and all my attention was on them.

This time, I was lucky to find some ex-pats to help me. 'Beirut Baby Mamas' was a mothers' group whose ten or so members met regularly at each other's homes or in public places such as bookshops. We did all the usual things: morning tea, picnics, makeshift splash pools, and plenty of chatting about raising children. Everyone was very supportive, and I always looked forward to our get-togethers. I never again wanted to feel as isolated and trapped as I did when Ali kept Lahela away from me and I spent those two soul-destroying weeks alone in our apartment with no one to turn to.

However, none of the mamas knew the personal issues I was battling. And it wasn't long after my return that one of those issues surfaced. It happened in the apartment. I had just hung out some washing on a balcony when Ali's mum unexpectedly walked in with some shopping. She looked at the washing and immediately shook her head and said in Arabic: 'No, this is no good.' Then she proceeded to take off all the washing and put it back in the basket before demanding that I re-hang everything. She left before she saw my second attempt, which was exactly the same as the first. I suspect she had no interest in how I did it; her whole reason seemed simply to irk me. And she succeeded.

I knew I could never hope to have a consistent relation-ship with Ali's mum. Our personalities were so different that clashes between us were always going to happen. Most of all, though, I believed that she would never approve of or accept me because I wasn't Lebanese. Rightly or wrongly, I imagined Ali's mum was often in my husband's ear, telling him I wasn't a suitable wife for him. Most of the time she made me feel I was an outcast, and that led to me yearning for home more than I ever had.

Ali knew how I felt. I had told him often that I was struggling and that I wanted to move back to Australia. Most of the time, when we talked about it we would end up fighting and I would get upset, which would see any constructive conversation end abruptly. One day, I sent Ali an email, trying to explain how I felt and why living in Lebanon wasn't working for me – or our marriage. I wanted Ali to understand how unhappy I was without getting emotional. Then, on 15 August 2013, that homesickness took on a whole new meaning.

Chapter Twelve

It was moments before sunset, another typical Mediterranean orange-and-red glow exaggerated by smog. Ali had just left the house to take Lahela to the movies, and I was about to put Noah to sleep in the kids' room. Then . . .

The noise was unmistakable. The boom went through my whole body, and Noah jolted in my arms. Suddenly car alarms shrieked all over the place. I'd never heard anything like it, but I immediately knew what it was.

I held my breath, and I don't think I breathed out for some time. I clutched Noah tightly and ran out of the bedroom, down the hall into the kitchen to a big window. I looked out and saw a huge black ball of smoke growing upwards into the sky only a few kilometres away.

A bomb.

Oh my God.

Lahela. Ali.

They were going in that direction. Towards the city centre. They would be near there. Right now.

I scrambled for my phone and called Ali. I couldn't get through, nor when I tried again. I had to put Noah down. He was crying because he was so tired, and maybe frightened by all of the noise outside. I dialled Ali again, but I still couldn't get through. I started to imagine horrible scenarios. My daughter. My husband. I picked up Noah and put him in a sling across my chest. I walked around the apartment, and kept going back to the kitchen window. All the smoke.

My fear grew as time went by. What could I do? Should I run out of the apartment and look for Ali and Lahela? I was scared at what I might find. Noah cried as sirens screamed.

I paced, trying again and again to get through to Ali and fighting to keep calm. Why didn't he answer his phone? I don't know how much time passed before there was a knock at the front door. I opened it and saw Ali holding Lahela, who was safe in her father's arms and oblivious to the drama that had occurred in the streets. I burst into tears.

'Oh my God, I thought you were dead.'

'Calm down, Sal. It's okay.'

'It's not okay! Look what's happened!'

'Calm down. Just breathe. Take a breath. Calm down.'

It took me hours to stop shaking and saying: 'I thought you were dead. I thought you were dead.' Ali tried to convince me that he and Lahela were never in danger because they'd gone in the opposite direction to the blast. But that did nothing to reassure me. They were on the streets, weren't they? And the streets could kill.

That evening, the city fell quiet again. I put the kids to bed and watched the television coverage of the blast. Twenty-seven people were killed and more than 200 injured. It was apparently an attack by Sunni militants against the Shi'ite Hezbollah, but different people claimed different things, and as always there were those who blamed Israel. I stared at the screen in disbelief. I was from Brisbane, for goodness sake. All the fear, unhappiness and insecurity about living in Beirut came to a head in that moment and I knew there was only one decision that could be made.

'Ali, I can't live like this.'

Ali ignored me.

'Ali!'

My husband looked straight at me. 'I heard you,' he said.

'Well, you haven't up to now. What are we going to do?'

'Hang tight, it'll pass.'

'Pass!'

'It's just one car bomb.'

'Just one car bomb! Right near us! The shop I get our groceries from is gone. The hairdresser is gone. People are dead. I heard it. I felt it!'

'Yeah, I get it.'

There was no emotion from him at all. I couldn't believe he was treating me like this again.

The kids and I didn't leave the apartment for the next week. Ali, though, went off to work, and he also got the groceries and water. I was scared to go out, terrified that another bomb would go off. Lahela was a good child who happily entertained herself, but by the end of the week she was getting very bored. She was three years old, she needed to be able to run and play and not be trapped inside an apartment for days on end. Going to Chakra wasn't an option. I'd become so anxious, I couldn't shake the fear and I doubted anything would settle me down, other than getting tickets back to Australia. Mum and Dad were worried and wanted Ali and me to get out with the children. In one conversation Mum was overwrought with worry, which Ali didn't appreciate.

The mood between Ali and me grew very tense. If I had only myself to consider, I may have contemplated staying, but a mere glimpse of Noah or Lahela was enough to tell me that the only sensible option we had was to leave. And leave soon. After another week of my constant pleading, Ali gave in, and I flew out of Beirut with the kids in late August.

As the plane took off, I thought to myself: *I can't come back here. I still want my marriage to work. But not here. Never here.*

If ever there was a moment to remind me of the questionable decisions I'd made during my marriage, it came soon after we touched down in Sydney. Lahela, Noah and I were waiting at a domestic boarding gate to connect to Brisbane when I noticed an old friend sitting close by. She didn't acknowledge the kids at all, and after a very brief exchange of nods and a couple of sharp words, she ignored me. We had once been really close mates – she knew much of my story – but she'd been angered by my choice to stay with Ali after he'd kept Lahela from me, and had given up on our friendship. In any domestic dispute there are a lot of people who are affected.

Although Ali didn't say much before I left, he must have known that our future was more uncertain than it had ever been. I had tried to talk to him so many times about it, so he knew how hard living in Lebanon without friends or family support was for me. He'd agreed to me returning to Brisbane and yet, the day after I arrived home, he rang to ask if the kids and I would come back in two weeks. The memories of that car bombing and the dread I felt wondering if Ali and Lahela were injured or worse were still too strong to think I could ever go back. But Ali persisted. He said I shouldn't get uptight about the bomb and that Beirut would soon be calm again. I didn't believe him. Hadn't his parents sent him to California when he was young for the same reasons? To be safe. I wanted my children to grow up in Australia because all parents want their children to be safe. I needed time to think, but at that moment I wasn't sure I could ever take the kids back to that fragile environment.

He didn't push me on the matter, but his intentions were clear. After that, we went into what you could say was a holding pattern. For the following few weeks we Skype-called every day, and I made sure he could speak with the kids. This, however, was easier said than done with Lahela because she was a little busy bee who flitted from one thing to the next, and as with most children her age, it was hard to sit her down and concentrate for any length of time. So, her conversations with Ali were generally short, but I made sure the camera was always on so he could watch her play while we talked.

As more days passed, my views on the future began to harden: I would never stop Ali from coming to Australia and spending time with the kids, but there was no way I could return to Lebanon. That just wasn't going to happen. So, where would that leave our marriage? Ali answered the question about a month after the kids and I returned to Brisbane.

'If we are not going to be in the same country, let's just separate. I think we should get a divorce.'

I felt both relieved and unbearably sad when he said that. To this day, I know I fought as hard as I could for our marriage, but everyone has a breaking point, no matter how tough or determined they are. This time, I didn't fight back against Ali's words. Our marriage had not been a healthy one. For so long I had been in denial about how much I had become dependent on Ali and all too quickly excused negative behaviour. I so desperately wanted my marriage to work I'd sacrificed my own sense of self-worth. I'd allowed a situation to develop that had cost me precious time with my daughter and I couldn't do that anymore. He was right. It was time to move on.

However, was there a catch? Later, when I reflected on what Ali had said, I began to wonder how serious he was. Was he trying to call my bluff? Had he expected me to say: 'No, no, I'll come back.' And when I didn't, what would he do? Would he follow through? He didn't. Instead, he came to Australia, and although he didn't push me about living in Lebanon, he flicked on the charm switch and told me how much he loved me and missed me.

I didn't fall for it this time. Something had changed in me and I wasn't going to put myself back in a position of weakness. If Ali moved to Australia we might have had a chance, but he wasn't going to do that. Living in Lebanon was impossible for me, it didn't feel safe and I was too isolated and alone. After everything that had happened, I was exhausted. I couldn't do it anymore.

I discussed with Ali how the kids were all that mattered now. I had seen first-hand how separated parents could respect each other and look after their children, and it was our responsibility to do the best by Lahela and Noah. Being in different countries would make our task much harder, but I knew we could do it. And if the kids could grow up having both of us in their lives, we would have something to be proud of as parents. I was surprised when Ali didn't protest. Perhaps he needed to hear me say everything to him face to face. This was, I thought, the biggest breakthrough. But then a greater one came when Ali acknowledged that his surf business was taking up so much of his time that I was the only one who could possibly be the primary carer of Noah and Lahela. He added that he would send money if I needed it, and he would visit whenever he could. I didn't consider his concession a victory at all; it was a matter of common sense that we would both contribute to the kids.

This all happened towards the end of 2013. Lahela was three and Noah had just turned one. I moved out of my mum's house – to give me a chance to develop my own mothering independence – and rented an apartment at Carseldine, about ten minutes' drive away. I was a single mum now, so I had to think about our future. For the very first time I felt I could settle, put down roots in the community and enjoy motherhood without any drama. I began to study for a Diploma of Early Childhood Education at a local TAFE institute, so life was going to be full.

At first, I was a little concerned about Lahela. She could worry about things that a little child needn't worry about; one of the most apparent of these was her ability to read how I felt, she was always very sensitive towards me when she sensed I was stressed. I wondered if her anxiety might have come from me – after all, throughout her entire life she'd had a mother who was generally unsettled and agitated, or missing. I thought I hid my jitters well from her, but I know now how children can pick up on even the smallest vibe; they are very perceptive. Thankfully, Lahela calmed down, and whether or not I was biased, I saw her become happier than she'd been in Lebanon. She, like every child, had her own peculiar traits. For a while she growled like a tiger then laughed whenever anyone picked her up or talked to her. It was cute, but sometimes I saw a few funny looks come our way as my tiger-child roared.

I discovered the joys of parenthood were often about the small, simple moments. Like buying Lahela a new bottle for bedtime. She was so excited that she carried it straight to her bed, drinking little sips as she went from the kitchen. She then placed it next to her on a table, and stared at it. Every now and again she'd pick it up, take a sip and say a contented 'Aaaaah!' at the end of each mouthful. Later on, she got into the habit of cuddling it in her sleep.

Bedtime was always a precious part of our day, especially when Noah grew a bit older and the interaction between us all became that much greater. I read at least one book every night. *The Pout-Pout Fish* was our favourite. It was about a fish that swam around with a pouty, dreary face that made all the other sea life ask why it didn't smile. The poor little Pout-Pout fish said it was just the way he was. But near the end of the story, Pout Pout got a smooch smooch from the Kiss-Kiss fish and realised he was a Kiss-Kiss fish too. Then he went around smooching and kissing all his friends in what was a very happy ending. Both of the kids loved it, especially Lahela who giggled at the rhymes, rhythms and funny illustrations.

Lahela could be a tough one to get to sleep; after books I quite often put on 'Twinkle Twinkle Little Star' from YouTube, and played it over and over again until the wriggling and banter stopped, and there was no sign of her eyes opening for a quick peep. I sang too, and some of the best tunes were ones that I made up as I went along. I look back now, and my God I miss those times. There was the chaos and craziness of cooking dinner, sitting the kids down to eat, and bathing them when more water seemed to end up on the floor than on their skin. Then came the sleep routine. Lahela and Noah each had their own bed, but only one was ever really needed. Sometimes Lahela would lie next to Noah and stroke his head until he nodded off. On other nights, they held hands and fell asleep within minutes of each other. So beautiful.

In the mornings, after breakfast, I would put them in a trailer that I could attach to my bike, and off we'd go for a ride, stopping to play at every playground along the route. On our way home we'd buy some fruit to juice together in what became our ritual start to the day. Then we'd head off to Gymboree or swimming lessons, visit family or friends, or do some craft at home. The days were busy but I loved every second I had with Lahela and Noah. As I said, simple moments.

Growing up happens too fast. Before I knew it, Noah had turned two and was mastering a scooter. He was a bit of a wizard who showed no fear for ramps at the local skate park. He was obviously a lot like his dad, and I look forward to one day telling Noah how I'd nicknamed Ali 'surfer guy' when I first saw him.

In a moment that shows how small the world has become in the age of social media, an American tourist took a photo of Noah scooting barefoot in a nappy, singlet and helmet, and being chased by me. The picture was put on Facebook, with a comment along the lines of 'This is what two-year-old Australians do.' The next thing I knew, a friend of a friend of mine saw it, and within a tag or two there was at least one person saying, 'Hey, that's Sally's boy!'

On another occasion I wanted to disown scooter boy when I was standing out the front of a school waiting for my mum to finish work. It was pick-up time, and there were a lot of parents about. Noah suddenly whizzed up behind me, jumped off his scooter, grabbed hold of my skirt and yanked it so hard that my underwear came down too. Mothers, particularly ones of little boys, learn to have good reflexes.

Certainly single-parenting has its headaches, but I can honestly say I rarely became frustrated or annoyed. Towards the end of finishing my early-childhood diploma I began to study as an external student for a degree in secondary education, with a science major.

I lost count of how many assignments I did at the Chipmunks play centre in Lawnton. Armed with a big bag of food – ham-and-cheese sandwiches, grapes, rockmelon, honeydew and the favourite go to, cucumbers – I would arrive in the morning and send Noah and Lahela off to play while I knuckled down to write. Because we went during the week there weren't many other children around, so it was easy to keep an eye on them, and hear where they were. They'd come back to me to eat, rest, cuddle or have the occasional tear wiped away, then they'd charge off again. We spent hours and hours there. I got my work done, and the kids had a ball.

The days blended into each other, and they were the best days of my life. I ensured Ali could see and speak with Lahela and Noah on Skype or by phone whenever he wanted. Contact was made most days. Then, every three months Ali would come out to spend time with the kids for about a fortnight, during which he'd either stay in my rented apartment, at my mum's place, or on the Gold Coast. He was so good with them, taking them away on trips up and down the coast, to fun parks, wildlife sanctuaries, playgrounds and play centres, the movies, all the usual places that families go. I sometimes went with them, and significantly, Ali and I got on better than we had at most stages of our marriage; this confirmed to both of us that we'd done the right thing by separating.

Throughout this period – leading up to the final months of 2014 – I was hanging out more with my friends, including Brendan, but our relationship was still platonic. When I knew things were finally over with Ali and I had settled back into the person I wanted to be rather than an anxious mess, I started to think that maybe there was something more there with Brendan. Who knew what would happen between us? All I wanted was for everyone in my life – including Ali – to be happy. Life felt good.

Part II

Chapter Thirteen

There are things that have happened in my life I doubt I'll ever be able to explain or understand. One of the weirdest occurred one night when I was putting Lahela and Noah to bed at my mum's place. Both were very nearly asleep when Lahela sat up and matter-of-factly said: 'There's Reginald.'

I was taken aback. Reginald was the name of Pa, mum's father, who died of a heart attack before Lahela was born. Mum and I had spoken about him to Lahela and Noah, but to my knowledge we never referred to him as Reginald; it was always Pa or the other name we knew him by, Jim.

'What did you say?' I asked Lahela.

'There's Reginald,' she repeated.

Then she looked straight at me and said: 'It's Jim. It's Jim.'

I felt a sudden rush of tingles.

'Where, Lahela?'

She pointed at the wall. The room was dark.

'Okay, sweetie, I'm just going to turn the light on for a second.'

The light came on, and we both looked at the wall.

'He's gone now,' said Lahela.

She lay down and was soon asleep, leaving me with serious goose bumps.

I don't know if I believe in ghosts, but that incident made me wonder. In all likelihood Lahela had heard 'Reginald' mentioned at some stage or other, and then, in her sleepy, dreamy head her imagination took over.

I wish my children had known all my grandparents. At the time we were living in Beirut, I was sorry that the problems Ali's mum and I had meant they didn't get to experience the unconditional love and fun grandparents can give very often. They are lucky, however, to have built wonderful relationships with many others among the older generations, including Mum and Dad and their partners and, as things became more serious between Brendan and me, with his parents, Greg and Barb, who live on the Gold Coast, an hour's drive from Brisbane. They didn't have any grandchildren at the time, so Lahela and Noah became much-loved substitutes. Barb, who happily suggested that she be called Nana, would play with the kids for hours. Hide-and-seek was a favourite. Two-year-old Noah, who was too young to grasp the finer details of the game, would hide with Nana Barb under the bed covers and chat away.

'Why are we here?'

'To hide from Lahela. Ssh, she's coming!'

'When's she coming?'

Then he'd pull the covers off to have a look just as Lahela came into the room.

Another time Lahela hid with Nana Barb in a spare bedroom, and although she was taking the game very seriously, she couldn't remain quiet.

'Goodness, this room is messy. Why is it so messy? And it's old too. Why is it so old? It's old and messy.'

Nana Barb couldn't help but laugh, which of course led Noah straight to them.

By late 2014 Barb and Greg had become part of my children's lives for one main reason: Brendan and I were becoming more serious. We weren't living together but we were now a couple and he was spending more time with me and the kids. When considering what would happen just a few months later, I now realise this was a critical time. I had no idea that Ali was getting angry. He never showed this to me and I, trustingly, was always honest and up-front about what was happening in my life. I felt I had to be because, no matter what, Ali and I were always going to be in each other's lives because we were parenting Lahela and Noah together.

I told Ali about my relationship with Brendan about a month before Christmas. Ali didn't say much, and maybe I should have worried but I didn't. He told me he'd decided to come to Australia to spend a couple of weeks with the kids either side of the New Year. I was happy to hear that, because I knew Lahela and Noah would love to see their dad. I wasn't expecting him to come over and try to convince me to get back together with him, but when he did I politely reinforced to him that our marriage was over, and also reminded him it was he who initially asked for a divorce. At that stage we'd been separated for about fourteen months. Ali appeared a little upset, but not angry.

On Christmas Day he joined the kids and me at my mum's place for a cheery morning of opening presents, then he took Lahela and Noah off to the Gold Coast for the start of their holiday. I went down later the same day because Brendan had invited me to stay with Barb and Greg. At the time I assumed everything was comfortable between Ali and me. I remember him ringing me one day and asking if I could have the kids while he went surfing. He wanted me to pick them up, but since he was borrowing my car, I insisted he drop them off. He picked them up a few hours later, but he refused to come inside to meet Brendan. I doubt I will ever know what he was really thinking when this happened.

I'm also never likely to know what Ali thought when Lahela started to talk about Brendan to him. Lahela got on really well with Brendan, and in the way any child can do so innocently, she chatted away happily, and expected Ali to be interested. However, from what I saw – and I judge the reactions more harshly with hindsight – Ali was always quick to turn the conversation in another direction, saying things like: 'Let's not talk about that. Daddy doesn't really like that guy.' I used to think, *Grow up, Ali. He's not trying to replace you.* But now I question if Ali was in fact boiling inside in ways I'd never imagined.

During that trip Ali and I had a few discussions about access and maintenance issues. We disagreed on a few things and I was very keen to sort them out by putting in place some sort of agreement between us. We had never made concrete rules about raising the children, but I thought it would only become a greater issue as more time passed, and a failure to have an understanding of what we could and couldn't do had the potential to cause great confusion and uncertainty, if not much worse. At times Ali mentioned he wanted to move to Australia, but he changed his mind so often it was difficult to know what he would actually end up doing. This uncertainty affected me because I never knew where the children and I really stood with him.

He returned to Lebanon in early January 2015, and came back to Australia less than a month later. Before he left again there was finally some clarity over our parenting when Ali and I sat down and had a frank discussion that resulted in

Ali writing a letter that laid down the outlines of what we had agreed. Among other things Ali agreed to 'always support' me in parenting. He would send me $600 a month, and a further $1000 every quarter as a buffer; and he would also provide further money if Lahela or Noah required something urgently. Much of the two-page letter detailed living matters. If Ali did move to Australia he would 'expect' me to give him fifty per cent access to the children. If he continued the current arrangement of visiting Australia whenever he could, he acknowledged he would provide a place for the children to stay with him away from my mum's house. Significantly, he wanted the kids to maintain 'healthy relations' with both sides of the family, which meant Lahela and Noah would visit Lebanon once a year. Despite still being anxious about tensions in Lebanon and the safety threats that could flare, I couldn't say no to that. I wanted the kids to know their grandparents and Lebanese relatives better, and without me there the reason for family dramas was removed, so it wouldn't be a problem for short holidays. And I told myself that Lahela and Noah would be in Chakra, not in the city. Now, as I look back on that letter, there are two other points that strike a powerful note:

> *'If at any point while Lahela or Noah are living with me* [sic] *decide that they want to live with their mom they can . . . make that call.'*

and

'If the children decide or mention that they are not happy with their current living situation because of a person in their household that is not family related then I expect a solution to be put in place or I can come and discuss a solution.'

I agreed to every point, and then with our custody parameters in place Ali and I simply got on with things on our respective sides of the world. For me, that meant more university studies. I had a very busy time ahead because at the end of April I was due to do a week of science prac work at Central Queensland University in Rockhampton, 600 kilometres north of Brisbane. I obviously needed help to look after the kids, so I asked Dad if he wanted some time away and could help me out. He was a workaholic, and I thought the break would do him good and give him a chance to spend some quality time with Lahela and Noah. Dad was up for it, which was great, but then Ali rang and announced that he wanted to come. I thought his timing was a little strange, and I must admit I didn't want it to seem as though we were going on a family holiday at a time when Brendan and I were very much together. I told Ali I didn't mind if he came, but I wondered if it was the best idea because Dad had already had his leave approved by his bosses, and we were all set. Ali, though, was adamant. So,

I rang Dad, and he didn't protest. He changed his plans, and that was that: Ali would come to Rockhampton with us.

He arrived in Australia a couple of days before my prac began. We drove up to Rockhampton and stayed in a caravan park. The region was still in a state of recovery after Cyclone Marcia had swept through two months earlier and caused widespread damage. Our days fell into a standard routine: Ali would drive me to the university campus at about 8am and pick me up at about 4pm. During the in-between hours he would take Lahela and Noah to parks, a play centre, and on riverside walks. There was a lot of outdoor play. At night, I would cook dinner, the kids would watch some TV cartoons, and Ali would reply to messages on his mobile phone. When it came time for sleep, Ali had the bed, and I wedged in between the children on mattresses on the floor. It was all very amicable, and I was actually pleased to see how relaxed Ali was. I was really pleased that we were getting on so well. Showing the kids that we were still united in loving and caring for them was very important to me.

Then came a real surprise when Ali asked if he could take Lahela and Noah back to Lebanon with him for two weeks. I wasn't prepared for that at all. I knew we'd agreed to a yearly visit in the letter Ali had written in February, but I assumed any such trip would have a considerable lead-up time. But this? All my fears came rushing back and I fought off the anxiety that came with them. My thoughts were racing. Ali and I had been getting on so well. He was being respectful, listening to me and taking on-board what I said. There were no problems, so how could I say no? I wanted to know what Lahela thought, so I dropped a question into general conversation when Ali wasn't with us.

'Would you like to go with Daddy to see Tata and Judo?'

Tata and Judo were what the kids called Ali's parents. Lahela said she wanted to go, but only if it was a holiday.

'Yes, a short one,' I said. 'Just a couple of weeks.'

I didn't ask Noah what he thought because he was too young to fully understand. He was more interested in riding his scooter, playing with his cars and doing the things that two-and-a-half-year-old boys do.

I thought hard about Ali's request for a day. It was like having a devil on one shoulder and an angel on my other. Should I? Shouldn't I? The memory of what Ali did to Lahela and me three-and-a-half years earlier was at the centre of my mind. I had never wholly trusted him since then, but I also understood the importance of upholding our agreement. I had to be fair to him and his family. To refuse the children the opportunity to spend time in Lebanon would have made me as cruel as Ali had been, and I didn't want that to happen. And, in all honesty, Ali could be wonderful with the children; at his best, he was a great dad. I couldn't rob Lahela and Noah of a bond with their father and his family. But, despite all the reasons that made some sort of sense for the children to go, my thoughts kept returning to the matter of trust. So, I put Ali on the spot.

'You look me in the eye and promise me that you will not do anything that—'

He stopped me before I could finish the sentence, and firmly reminded me he'd said many times that he wouldn't repeat what had happened with Lahela. He promised me. I continued to look at him, refusing to break eye contact.

'That is a promise, Ali. You're promising me?'

'Yes, I promise.'

'Are you sure?'

'Look, I don't even want to have this conversation. If we're going down that road again, we'll just forget about it, and the kids can stay here. I don't want to relive that.'

He threw in a few expletives. It was obvious he was getting angry.

I told him I didn't want to start an argument, but I had to remind him what a devastating experience losing access to Lahela had been, for her and for me. He replied by saying that he didn't have the time to look after the kids full-time because he had a business to run.

'As long as you promise, I believe you,' I said.

And that was the end of the discussion.

Everyone stayed at my mum's place the night before departure. I woke up early in the morning, and sneaked into the kids' bedroom and took a photo of Ali asleep next to Noah. I stared at my son for a long time; his eyes opened every now and then, but soon he was back fast asleep, and I was left thinking to myself: *Two weeks. That's all they'll be away from me for.* Ali and I had agreed that I would travel to Beirut to pick them up and bring them home. Two weeks wasn't long. I could manage that, couldn't I?

I then went downstairs and played with Lahela, who was already up. All too soon, Ali came down with Noah and the luggage. I drove them to the airport mid morning. Ali was really bubbly and the mood in the car was cheerful. At a set of traffic lights I turned around and looked at the kids happily swinging their legs.

'I'm going to miss you guys soooooooo much,' I said.

'And we're going to miss you sooooooo much,' replied Lahela.

I turned to Ali and reminded him of his promise. He made a clicking sound as though admonishing me while he stared straight ahead.

When we arrived at the airport I hugged Lahela and Noah, and buried my nose in their hair and took deep breaths.

'Mummy loves you so much.'

Again I turned to Ali. 'You look after them.'

'Of course I will.'

'I'll miss them.'

'I'm sure they'll miss you too.'

Surprisingly, Ali then hugged me and told me I was a good mum.

'Thank you, and you're a good dad.'

Then I watched them walk away, Lahela and Noah both with their little backpacks on, and full of bounce. It was Friday, 22 May 2015.

I told myself I wasn't going to cry. Two weeks. That's all it was. Then I would go over, see them and then bring them home.

Two weeks.

I'd barely left the airport when my phone rang.

'Sally, I fuckin' told you.'

My heart started to pound. Ali had been pulled aside at the immigration checkpoint because the kids' names had come up on a watchlist that was connected to the court order I'd taken out after the episode with Lahela. Prior to Ali leaving I'd checked that the order was no longer in date, and assured Ali he wouldn't have any worries. However, officials still stopped him and wanted to speak with me. I felt bad. I told them there were no problems, and I planned to go to Beirut in two weeks' time to pick up Lahela and Noah. They allowed Ali to go through. He got back on the phone and apologised for being rude to me and blamed his outburst on a sudden rush of panic because he thought he and the kids would miss their flight. I told him to calm down, but at the same time, I began to worry. I had seen that sudden flash of anger that had been so much a part of his personality during the time we were together. I convinced myself that it was a rare lapse, because for the past twenty-one months – the period I'd had Lahela and Noah in Brisbane – Ali had been relaxed and respectful most of the time. A few times he'd brought up the subject of Brendan – which I understood because it is hard when a marriage ends and someone new on the scene highlights the finality – but never in an angry way, so I had no reason to think there were any serious issues brewing.

My faith in the 'new Ali' was restored almost immediately when I received some happy selfies of him, Lahela and Noah from on board the plane before take-off. They made me laugh, and I felt better. Then, I got some more after Ali and the kids had landed to change flights in Singapore. I sent a message back to them, saying I'd speak to them soon after they arrived in Beirut. So far, so good.

But, just a day later . . .

How could I have been so trusting again, after all he'd done?

Chapter Fourteen

Lahela and Noah were still asleep when Ali Skype-called me from the apartment in Beirut. I was at Brendan's apartment sitting on the living-room couch. Brendan was in the kitchen.

'How are you going?' I asked.

'Good.'

It was a worryingly short answer. My heart skipped a beat.

'Are you all right, Ali? Are you still tired from the flight?'

'Yeah.'

'How was the trip?'

'Good.'

Something was obviously wrong. The cold tone and meaningless answers were one thing, but the more troubling sign was the fact that Ali wasn't looking at the screen camera; he was looking anywhere but at me. Then, he was. Those flat, emotionless eyes stared straight down the camera at me.

'Sal, plans have changed.'

'What do you mean?'

I already knew what he was going to say. I felt my whole body tense up.

'The kids are staying here. They're not going back to Australia.'

'What do you mean? You can't do this. What about your promise? You *promised*, Ali. You can't do this again! I trusted you, Ali.'

Those eyes. Those horrible eyes. That look. Ali had shut himself off from me. I felt as though I was going to be sick. I could barely get a word out, and then all of a sudden I heard Lahela's voice.

'Is that Mummy? Is that Mummy?'

Oh my God, I couldn't let her see me like this. I was crying and shaking. Trembling.

I hung up. Brendan found me and tried to reassure me, saying Ali was just going through one of his moments.

'I don't think he is. This is pre-meditated,' I said.

I calmed myself down for a short while, and then rang back and asked to speak with Lahela.

'Hi Mummy.'

'Hello, sweetheart. Did you have a good trip?'

'Yes, it's a good holiday so far.'

Those few little words rocked me. I felt the tears come again. I could only think that Lahela would soon believe that I'd lied to her. This wasn't a holiday.

'Mummy, have you been crying? Are you okay?'

'Yes, sweetheart, I'm okay.'

'No, you're not. You're going to cry. What's wrong, Mummy?'

I pulled the laptop down, and tried to piece myself together. It was only for a few seconds, and when I opened up the computer again Ali was in the background of the screen, watching and listening. Lahela looked a little worried.

'Hello, sweetheart. I'm so happy to see you. You know sometimes Mummy cries when she is really happy? Right now, I am just so happy. I love you so much.'

By then, Noah had woken up and I heard him somewhere out of sight behind Lahela.

'Mummy, we went on a big plane.'

I had to cry.

I had to.

I was trying so hard to forget what Ali had just said to me. I tried to convince myself that he was just having one of his moments, and at any time he would come back on and talk to me about travel arrangements for the kids to return home. Meanwhile, Lahela was excitedly telling me about everything she planned to do on the 'holiday', and what she wanted to bring back to Australia. It was shattering.

I hung up. Brendan looked at me and said: 'He can't do that. He just wouldn't do that again, Sally.'

I ran down the hallway and collapsed on the floor. Brendan came after me and picked me up. Brendan had never seen me cry like this before. He hugged me and took me back to the living room. I was a mess. No one could console me. I got so worked up that I went and threw up in the toilet, and bawled with my head in the bowl. I couldn't stand up. If I had called Ali back at that moment, I knew he wouldn't have cared. He would have thrived on seeing me at my lowest; I believe it would have made him feel better about what he'd done.

After I'd regained some composure I rang my mum, but her reaction only set me off again. We shared our tears down the line, and I again felt too weak to move.

* * *

I couldn't sleep for the next two nights. It was as though I'd been told that Lahela and Noah were dead. How else was I to react to having the two most precious people in my world stolen from me? It was the most heart-wrenching time of my life and I instantly had the same sense of dread I'd carried when Ali took Lahela from me the first time. How could he do this again? I don't know how I kept going but amid the despair came an unexpected twist that hit me as utterly surreal. Just four days after Ali's revelation, I had a quiet announcement of my own that I had to make to Brendan: I was pregnant.

I told him in a coffee shop. In his happy eagerness to hug me he knocked stuff all over our table. He kept saying: 'Oh my God, really?' His reaction was such a warming contrast to the ones I'd had with Ali at similar times. However, I was confused, to say the least. We had talked of children and I knew that this was something we'd both wanted, but not so soon. Of course I was happy, but any excitement I had was dulled by everything else that was happening to me. My emotions were like a rolling ball covered in different themes: happiness, sadness, anger, frustration, desperation, fear . . . I went through them all.

I think Brendan was immediately worried that I could potentially miscarry because of all the stress I was under. As a result, after his initial reaction, he calmed down; considering the context of the pregnancy, this was a time to provide more support and understanding than most men would ever have to give their expectant partners. It was, in many ways, a very difficult position for Brendan to be in. It was also a challenge for me because I had to ride my hormones; share the joy of celebrating a new, growing life with the man I loved, and yet try to come to terms with the loss of my other two children and fight to bring them home.

It is fair to say, Lahela and Noah took up more of my thoughts. At first, I grieved. Then, I went into a period of denial. My family and friends offered as much support as they could. There were many reassurances. No one could believe that Ali would follow through. Those who'd met him thought he'd been friendly and supportive while the kids had been with me in Australia. I thought that as well, but I also knew his other side, a side most people didn't get to witness.

About a week after Ali told me of his plans, I completely fell apart. At the time I was working at an early-childhood centre, and also continuing my education studies. I no longer cared about either of them. I didn't want to get out of bed. I didn't want to do anything. That's when my parents stepped in together. Dad came to Mum's place and the three of us had a long talk.

'You have to be strong, love,' said Dad.

I wasn't in the mood for a pep talk. I told him to 'get stuffed', and angrily questioned why he would want me to 'get over it'.

'I'm not telling you to do that at all, Sally. Just look at it. You *must* be strong. Your kids love you, and they *will* come back. You need to be that strong someone to come back to.'

But I didn't want to listen to him. I wanted to grieve for as long as I liked. I wanted to be left alone. My only aim was to speak with the kids at least once a day, so I tried to contact Ali frequently, sometimes several times a day. I knew that would annoy him, and my constant pleas to change his mind would have antagonised him more. Looking back, maybe I should have given him more space. But I was desperate.

No matter how hard I tried, I wasn't able to speak with Lahela and Noah very often. It took only a few days for me to realise that Ali wasn't spending much time with them. Before he left he'd told me his business was taking up a lot of his time, and it seemed that having Lahela and Noah with him hadn't changed that. Instead, he would go to work – or for a surf – and leave his mother to look after them in the apartment. The few conversations I had with the children during those times were very distressing to me. I tried not to let Lahela know that. On the worst Skype-call of all, Lahela said to me: 'We're lonely. Daddy leaves us all the time with Tata, and she doesn't know what we're saying, and she gets angry when I ask for a cucumber. I'm hungry now but I don't know what to say.'

She asked me when I was going to come to get her and Noah. At that stage they didn't know they weren't returning to Australia, and I couldn't find the words; I didn't want to lie, nor did I want to tell the truth. Either way could hurt.

'Sweetheart, Mummy really wants to come and get you, and hopefully I will see you soon.'

I knew Lahela sensed that something was wrong, and she was becoming agitated. She again said she was hungry and wanted a cucumber.

'Maybe you can go and get Tata and I can ask her for you?'

'No, she's busy.'

At about that point Noah, who looked bored, started to poke Lahela, and she began to cry.

'Where's Daddy?' I asked.

'He left very early.'

I was furious.

Hearing Lahela, Ali's mother came across to her and asked what was wrong.

'She's lonely and misses her mum,' I blurted out. 'I can't believe you're doing this. This is *not* okay. This is *not* normal.'

It was obvious that she didn't understand me. She looked at me and intimated that Lahela was fine before the Skype call with me.

'She's crying because she misses me!' I shouted.

In the background Noah started to scream.

Tata hung up.

I wanted to reach through the screen, hug my children tight and pull them to safety. But . . . Do you know what the definition of utter helplessness is? It is seeing your children broken and sad, and realising you can't do anything to help them. At that moment Ali's mother had all the power. And she only had to push a button to prove it.

Fighting back tears, I called Ali's mobile, but it took a number of attempts before he answered. He'd been in the surf. I told him what had just happened, and accused him of spending time catching waves when he should have been with the children. He said he'd been working. I had my doubts because he had two other employees who could conduct lessons; he didn't need to be there, especially when he'd brought his two children halfway around the world and put them in an apartment for hours on end with an elderly woman who could not speak their language.

'You're messing with their heads!' I said.

'Sal, what do you want me to do?'

'I want you to go home and spend time with our children. They need you.'

'I'll see them later.'

And then, *he* hung up.

For the next few days I tried every way I knew to contact Ali – Skype, WhatsApp, email, phone, text message – but he wouldn't answer. Finally, I heard from him: he said I could try Skype-calling the kids on their iPad. On about the third attempt I got through. Lahela answered, and she seemed a little happier than our last conversation, but she was still missing home and said she badly wanted to be back with me. Noah then got on.

'When are you coming to get us, Mummy?'

I avoided the question, and asked what he'd been doing.

'Mummy, I miss you. When are you coming to get us?' he repeated.

'Sweetie, I don't know. You'll have to ask Daddy.'

That triggered tears from both of them. We were all crying by the end of the call. Immediately afterwards, Ali rang me – he'd presumably been contacted by his mother – and accused me of upsetting the children. We argued. I said it was disgraceful that he could say one thing and do another in front of the children; there had to be repercussions for his actions. He simply hit back with the same line again and again: I was the one making the kids cry. We were getting nowhere until Ali showed *his* power: 'If you're going to make the kids cry, you're never going to talk to them again.'

I went quiet.

'I've got to go,' he said, and hung up.

Over the following days, I sent Ali many messages asking when I could talk to the kids again. He didn't answer directly – instead, he sent me an awful video recording that showed Noah and Lahela walking in and out of shot while Ali, off camera, asked: 'Do you want to talk to Mummy?' Both children said, 'No.' (Early in the clip, Ali's father could be heard off camera saying 'No' as though prompting Lahela and Noah.) Noah stared blankly and dropped toys; he and Lahela were being used as puppets. I sensed that Ali was almost daring them to say yes. It was very, very disturbing. I felt ill, and was petrified about what might happen next. Ali was using Lahela and Noah to hurt me, and any tiny bit of trust I had in him was shattered. He didn't seem to care that he was denying me contact. He was, however, true to his word in one sickening way: he stopped the children from talking to me.

I was only beginning to know what loneliness can feel like.

Chapter Fifteen

Two weeks after saying goodbye to Lahela and Noah, I no longer had any contact with them. I bombarded Ali with messages, but it was no use. I contemplated flying to Beirut, but that was fraught with danger. For one, I was pregnant, and with Ali in such a vindictive mood, who knows what he might have done after I arrived. Technically we were still married, and I didn't know if under Lebanese law he had the authority to prevent me from leaving again. I was hoping he would soon reconsider and I knew that if I just turned up and knocked on his door that would inflame things. Ali had all the power. I had none.

Despite my despair, I began to realise the importance of my dad's previous words to me. He was so right. I had to be strong.

For the rest of 2015 I became intensely absorbed by the need to raise awareness about the situation that my children and I were in; I now know what people mean when they say they have found their passion in life. One of the first things I did was to launch a public Facebook page called 'Bring Lahela and Noah home'.

I explained what had happened to my children, and drew attention to the fact that Lebanon is not a member of the Hague Convention. I added that in Lebanon, Lahela, Noah and I don't have any rights, but I wasn't about to give up our fight any time soon. I invited all my friends to join, and asked them in turn to invite others. Within a few weeks I had 3000 people in the group, and it continued to grow.

I also rang the Department of Foreign Affairs and Trade (DFAT) in Canberra. I was made aware of a bilateral agreement between Australia and Lebanon, but in the same conversation I was also told that this was basically a fancy term for mediation, and unless Ali was willing to come to the table, it was a waste of time. I argued that my problem was an international problem because it involved another country, but basically, the implication was that I was involved in a domestic issue that didn't fall within the department's responsibility. DFAT did, however, start a file on my family and recommended I contact the Department of Communities, Child Safety and Disability Services. After doing this, I quickly learned that there were hundreds of other people in similar positions to me, and my chances of having any success in retrieving my children from a non-Hague country were minimal, unless Ali changed his mind.

Of course, I had to try everything I could, so I employed a legal firm to begin the long process of applying through the Family Law Court for sole parental responsibility. I was advised that my being granted custody would mean nothing in Lebanon, but it was, nevertheless, a potentially important document if Ali ever brought Lahela and Noah back to Australia.

Facebook, DFAT and the law were all predictable channels for me to explore. But there was a fourth, which was much more intimidating, and one I knew nothing about: child recovery. I came across it during one of my countless sessions trawling the Internet for even the tiniest of loopholes or opportunities. One of the first organisations I came across was Child Recovery Australia, and soon enough I was speaking with specialist Col Chapman. Sadly, he told me how common child abductions across the world are. We also discussed general details about recovery operations. Col was very thorough and helpful. Yet, when I got off the initial call with him, I felt sick and very angry. How could right-minded people allow such horrible things to be done to our children? Why weren't governments more concerned about the issue? Child abduction destroys lives.

I ended up speaking with Col a number of times. He became like a counsellor to me, a source of some comfort because he knew as well as anyone what the kids and I were going through. He also knew the ins and outs of government regulations, different cultures and behaviours. I learned a lot from him. And I grew to trust him.

In July, six weeks after Ali had taken the children, my aim for widespread awareness gained a lot of momentum after a producer from Channel Nine's *A Current Affair* (*ACA*) program contacted me on Facebook and arranged to do a story about me.

I was with Brendan in his apartment on the evening the piece went to air. His flatmate and one of my closest friends, Dana, were also there. Within minutes of the broadcast my iPhone started to ping non-stop until it went into a glitch and turned itself off. By the time I was able to turn it on again, I had hundreds of messages: texts, Facebook and Instagram posts, Instant Messenger notes – my phone was inundated.

The general comments were full of support, sympathy and shock. It took me some time to determine how legitimate and genuine others were, such as people who insisted they knew someone who knew someone who knew how to get the children out. One person sent me a 24-page email.

At that time I hadn't heard from Ali for quite a while, despite my continuous attempts to contact him and the children, but that changed dramatically after the *ACA* story.

It didn't take long for him to contact me on WhatsApp. He was furious, and reinforced that there was no way I would ever speak with Lahela and Noah again if I kept saying he had kidnapped the children. Furthermore, he blocked me on all of his social media sites. But *ACA* had revealed Ali's business page on Facebook, and Surf Lebanon had apparently been smashed with angry messages that suddenly forced Ali into damage control; I could only imagine the effect that a flood of derogatory remarks could have on his reputation and that of his business. For a brief moment, I felt sorry for him. I doubted that many people who knew him were actually aware of the truth behind Lahela and Noah being with him, but I hoped they would find out and maybe, just maybe, Ali would realise what he was doing was wrong.

The *ACA* story also prompted a number of child-recovery agencies to contact me. Some had already done so through Facebook, and the more responses I got, the more I realised how big a demand there was for this line of work. I hoped that I would never have to go down that track, but the possibility was growing in my thoughts. If Ali was blocking all contact, what else could I do but go and get my children myself? The average cost to conduct an operation was about $100 000, and some agencies quoted as much as $150 000. It was a world I had never known about and the money was mindboggling, but I thought of Lahela and Noah asking when I was coming to get them. I thought of their tears and asked myself, could you ever put a price on your children's happiness?

The most unexpected reaction from the *ACA* story remains very clear in my memory. I hadn't long begun a new job at an early-childhood centre when a mother approached me.

'My God, please tell me you're not the girl I saw in that interview. Your children. It can't be you.'

I burst into tears, and in the middle of a little playground, this complete stranger hugged me. She showed a lot of concern for me, and apologised if she'd embarrassed me. The director of the centre was standing near us, and saw and heard the whole exchange. I hadn't told her my history when I accepted the job only weeks earlier.

'What interview? What's this all about?' she asked.

I was emotionally exhausted, and was quite content to let the mother tell the story. Later, the director spoke with me privately. She was very supportive, and stopped me worrying that I might lose my job.

Working at the childcare centre was such a bittersweet experience. To see gorgeous children missing their mums and dads for a whole day was sometimes hard to handle, and I found myself cuddling many of them, and it got to the point that I was nearly always carrying someone around throughout the day. Occasionally the kids would push and shove each other to have their turn with me; I didn't encourage that behaviour, but admittedly, there were times when I actually felt humbled by it because it showed me how much I could be wanted by a child.

Humbled.

And sad.

There was one girl who had big brown eyes like Lahela and Noah. She used to ask me to brush her hair, and one day as I was plaiting it, I started to cry. Whenever I walked into the centre to start work, I never quite knew what to expect, nor did I know how I would be by the end. Throughout it all, Lahela and Noah were there with me; I carried photos of them in my pockets, and not an hour went by without me stopping for a quiet moment to sneak a look at the pictures, which I changed from day to day. Generally, I dared not look at them for any more than a handful of seconds; any longer, and I risked breaking down.

Wherever I went, Lahela and Noah came too. In their snug, protective places they were witnesses to some unpredictable outbursts from their highly strung mother. There were times I was so focused – such as when I sat down to sift through emails concerning legal matters – that my emotions didn't come into play at all, but there were other instances when simple everyday activities triggered me.

One morning I was in a post office, standing in a queue behind a man carrying a child. As I looked at the child's head my thoughts drifted off and I was soon imagining Lahela and Noah running into the post office yelling,

'Mummy! Mummy!' while behind Ali came in saying, 'I'm sorry.' I snapped back into reality when I felt tears well up, and then an old man with a walking stick moved past and smiled gently at me. That was all it took for the tears to flow. I turned around and ran out of the post office.

On another occasion I was in a supermarket queue when the mother in front of me began to lose patience with her daughter who was throwing a tantrum on the floor. The screams got louder, and so did the mother's demands that the child get up. Eventually, the mother grabbed the girl's arm and roughly pulled her to her feet, but the child went limp and fell back to the floor. This happened a few times, each time the screaming and demands growing louder, until I too became angry and burst out: 'You don't know how lucky you are to have that child! And here you are treating her like a bag full of groceries.'

'Excuse me?' said the mother.

'You heard what I said. It's wrong. You don't do that.'

The mother turned back to the child and again told her to get off the floor, but nothing happened. Then I stepped in and softly said to the girl: 'Maybe you should go with Mummy because Mummy's about to leave.' The girl looked at me with some bewilderment – as you could expect when a request came from a stranger – but she then stood up and followed her mother out. Meanwhile, I knew others nearby were looking at me and possibly wondering who the crazy woman was. Perhaps I was a hormonal mess because of my pregnancy, or maybe it was jealousy of someone who had something I didn't. I snapped out of the rage and felt so self-conscious that I apologised to the check-out operator. Her response surprised me: 'Don't worry, we get them all the time.' I left the store wondering whether it was my type or the mother's type who were so common.

We all judge others in various ways. That's human nature. Being forced to live without Lahela and Noah has made me a lot more judgmental of parents than I'm sure I would have been if I had my children with me all the time. If they did return right now and they threw a wobbly on a supermarket floor, I think I'd chuckle a bit. Why? Because I'd just be so grateful to have them. I've heard it said that it's not until you lose something that you appreciate its true value. That's not the case with children, because the richness they bring to every day you are with them is priceless. However, when they aren't with you, the memories you have of them become so much more valuable. To this day, what tears me up most about this whole disaster is the knowledge that I'm never again likely to be with Lahela and Noah during their childhoods, and that means I'll miss a huge piece of their lives – perhaps their whole lives – when I won't be able to show them how much I love them. So, a tantrum on a supermarket floor? I'd give anything to be next to any of my children if they had one.

Episodes like the ones at the supermarket and the post office sometimes launched me into periods of intense reminiscence. Noah's laugh echoing in my head; Lahela's serious tone; Noah's blue scooter and matching blue skate shoes; Lahela's art and craft; Noah's sandy brown cowlick; Lahela carefully choosing the vegetables for our morning juice; Noah using a hand signal I taught him to tell me he was thirsty, long before he could talk . . . all random snippets of innocent lives. I missed going with the kids to Thursday playgroup at the local church. I missed going to a beach to collect shells. I missed the afternoons at the skate park where Noah would zoom off and Lahela and I would sit on a picnic blanket and bead bracelets. I missed Chipmunks, where Noah would wear a pair of Lahela's tights so he wouldn't get slide-burn. I missed so much. What I missed most of all was being their mum.

Nights were generally the worst for me. They still are. They made me think of lying next to the kids and tickling their heads until they drifted off. Quite often I used to have Lahela lying on one of my arms, and Noah across the other; my hands would get pins and needles but I dared not move them until all was quiet. Even in silence and darkness, a parent lying next to their child surely can't help but be overcome by love.

Although I was trapped in my own nightmare, I realised others in my close circle were also struggling in their own ways. Mum was the obvious one. One day, when in the middle of teaching in a classroom, she stopped, walked out, went to the principal and said she couldn't handle the situation any longer. As a result, she had to take time off work. Dad, meanwhile, swayed between denial, anger and arguments with me during which he suggested it was time for me to rebuild and accept there was nothing I could do. Brendan's parents, Barb and Greg, were furious – Barb cried a lot – and my stepdad, Lew, also had his moments; he and I had had more than a few issues with each other over the years, but I always respected him. He was attached to my children and was always patient whenever he was cornered to answer the most ridiculous of questions. Simon went into denial for a long time; he used to see Lahela and Noah nearly every day, and one of Lahela's favourite times was going over to Uncle Simon's for a movie and a sleepover. It wasn't until much later that I found out just how badly my brother had been affected.

My twelve-year-old half-brother Bryce had been more of a brother to the kids than an uncle; he copped a few things in the back of his head and was both the tormented and tormentor in household and playground games. I didn't ever see him cry in front of me about Lahela and Noah, but Mum said she'd seen him shed a few tears. And he also did something rather unusual: after Mum first told him the kids weren't coming back, he started to sleep anywhere but in his own bed. On Lew's boat, in a tent, in the lounge room on the couch, downstairs on a mattress. Even now, he still does it.

In addition to handling the pain of the children's absence, everyone had to put up with me. I often became frustrated by the most insignificant things, such as someone whingeing about the wind or the taste of a chicken sandwich. I could snap at them without warning, but as the weeks went by I forced myself to stop talking about these frustrations because I didn't want to drive my friends away. However, there were two who didn't mind how I behaved. Dana and Sacha were always willing to listen. They'd been there from the start of our Emirates days, and both had since moved on and were based in Queensland. I probably didn't appreciate the true worth of their support at the time, but I do now.

And of course, there was Brendan. I don't know how he managed to stay with me. I no longer laughed at his jokes and I rarely even smiled at him. Day in, day out, he copped the worst. Day in, day out, he was there for me. Such a strong man. He loves Lahela and Noah very much. In the evenings, when he came to visit them, he would wrestle with Noah, or play airplanes with both children, holding them above his head and flying them around the room to fits of laughter. They were such joyful moments, the moments that any child needs to have, but, as I will discuss later, I now know how destructive those moments were.

So, there were many people in my nightmare. And as time passed, more and more came in and out. Not long after the *ACA* story, we held a fundraiser on the Gold Coast. Nearly 100 people turned up on the night, and bought everything from little yellow ribbons at one dollar each to a quilt that Mum made, which fetched $1000, and a painting that went for twice as much. In all, about $8000 was raised to help cover my mounting legal costs. I was extremely touched by everyone's kindness. When you're going through a traumatic experience, you can often feel very alone and think that no one fully understands the intense emotions you grapple with, but when people get together to collectively show how much they care, that loneliness is put into the corner and forgotten – at least for a while. There were friends and family, my solicitor, and many people I'd never met who simply believed in the cause and wanted to help reunite me with Lahela and Noah.

The evening was also what you could call my 'coming out', because I was just beginning to show a baby bump. Until then, next to no one knew, apart from Brendan's parents and mine. I was on such an emotional rollercoaster I didn't tell anyone else, which became an issue after Simon sat down at the main table and was innocently asked by Barb: 'So, do you think it will be a boy or a girl?' Simon looked quizzically at Mum, who confirmed another child was on the way. Simon was so taken aback that he got up and walked off. He returned later, but for the following few days he was standoffish towards me. Understandably, he needed time to process my pregnancy in the context of everything else that was happening.

Unfortunately, throughout all this time, there was no positive news from Lebanon. Ali continued to ignore me, and the only knowledge I had of the children's welfare was through photos that my friends had access to on Ali's Facebook page. Nothing was changing. All I could do was keep agitating from Australia and hope that the next day would finally be different from the last.

And that day finally came. But not in a way I would ever have expected.

Chapter Sixteen

As I've said, I want my kids to know I never stopped fighting to see them, to talk to them, to bring them back to me. The sixteenth of November 2015 was one of the most important days for me since Ali had told me that Lahela and Noah weren't coming back to Australia. I left home in the morning with my stomach churning.

'What do you think will happen?' asked Mum.

'I don't know.'

About two weeks earlier I'd been told I had a court hearing for 16 November, but I had been forced to ask my solicitor if it could be adjourned; I'd been in and out of court several times over the past six months, and my debts were rising – I simply didn't have the money I needed. However, my solicitor was convinced this would be the last time I would have to appear, and we came to an arrangement that if I could secure the finances to pay off the barrister for the day, then I could pay the remaining fees at a later time. So, I went into a frantic borrowing mode, and thankfully Mum, Dad, Simon and Brendan all came to the rescue with the $4500 I needed.

I arrived at the Family Law Court feeling numb; all the adrenaline and emotion over the past few months had left me empty, and I just couldn't work myself up to hope for a new result. Dana sat behind me in the public area. She'd made an extraordinary effort to be there for me; only a few hours earlier she'd flown into Sydney from Dallas, before she caught a connection to the Gold Coast and then hopped in her car to drive to Brisbane.

After the registrar made her announcement I still didn't feel as excited as I would have expected; sure, I felt tears, but it took a while for the decision to sink in. I was awarded sixteen orders, every single one that I'd wanted. Among them: I was granted sole parental responsibility for Lahela and Noah; I could obtain Australian passports in which I was the sole signatory for them; a recovery order stated that Ali must return the children to me; a restraining order stated that Ali could not again remove them from my care without the appropriate consent; and the names of Lahela and Noah would be added by the Australian Federal Police to the Family Law Watchlist.

I had heard Dana burst into tears as the announcement was made, and as we hugged afterwards outside the
courtroom, she kept saying, 'It's okay, Mumma, you're going
to get your kids back.'

She also pulled out a little car she'd found outside the
building's lifts.

'Look, this is an omen. When you get them back you can
give Noah this. You've won!'

I believed Dana. I *had* to believe this was going to make
a difference. Yes, I had won and I would have my children
again. It didn't matter that the orders wouldn't be recognised
in Lebanon; this was a step in the right direction. And Ali
would know about it too, because the court held off on its
announcement until papers had been personally delivered
to him in Beirut. This had been a difficult process, because
the lawyer I'd hired to do that had tried unsuccessfully over
several weeks; at times I suspected Ali had point-blank denied
his identity to the lawyer, causing enough confusion for the
lawyer to leave without handing over the documents.

This prolonged process revealed a telling difference
between the Australian and Lebanese courts. Whereas the
Australian system wouldn't grant the orders without the
father being notified, I learned much later that Ali had
sought and been awarded custody of the children, without
my knowledge, through a Lebanese religious court. I was
told by my Lebanese lawyer that he claimed I'd abandoned

the children. That was not true, and Ali knew this. It didn't stop him falsely presenting this allegation to the court. I had no knowledge of any of this and no opportunity to contest Ali's claims. My estranged husband may not have cared less when he read the Australian orders, but at least I could make him aware that I was fighting him and would never give up.

Up until that point, the legal process had cost me about $45 000. Every cent I'd been able to save went towards lawyers' bills. Mum, who'd been worried about my mounting debts, was relieved when I told her I'd got the orders. This time there were no tears. She knew I had, *we had*, still a very long way to go.

So, what next?

A woman named Samantha from the online petition service Change.org contacted me and arranged to film and post a video and petition in a bid to attract the attention of Australia's Foreign Affairs Minister, Julie Bishop. I can't recall exactly the timing or sequence of interviews, because the days were a blur, but at about this time I was also contacted by, and appeared on, Channel Nine's *Today* show and *The Project* on Channel Ten. Ever since Ali took the children I had periodically been interviewed by various media outlets, which kept awareness of my campaign bubbling along, but there was still the obvious problem: it was all great keeping the issue somewhere in the public eye, but how could it bring Lahela and Noah back to Australia?

I didn't have a plan. I could get court orders, hire a Lebanese lawyer, do interviews, answer emails, apply for passports, be hugged and given hope by friends and family, and keep begging Ali to change his mind. I could do all of that and more, but would there come a point when I would have to accept that there was nothing more that could be done?

It was an up-and-down time because the birth of Brendan's and my baby was getting close. Unfortunately, this pregnancy hadn't run smoothly. On many mornings I found it difficult to get out of bed. I was exhausted and didn't feel well. The fact that I was still working added to my tiredness. I didn't know what was wrong; at first I put it down to stress and grief. I have to admit I wasn't as vigilant about looking after myself because so much was going on. Finally, the doctor diagnosed me with hypothyroidism, which is a low-functioning thyroid, and I was put on medication that helped a lot. But I still carried the weight of sorrow at Lahela and Noah's absence and it sucked the joy out of everything.

Meanwhile, Brendan had bought a block of land on which we planned to build a home, and in a way of saving money, he had moved out of his flat and in with me at Mum's place. While Lahela and Noah were at the centre of our thoughts, we all knew a new baby would bring a change of focus and priorities.

Then, out of the blue, I received a phone call from a freelance journalist who asked if I was interested in doing a story with the *Sunday Night* program on Channel Seven. I had become used to such requests, and had no worries about doing them because they all served the purpose of creating exposure for my cause and those of other parents in similar positions to me. I had a couple of follow-up conversations with the journalist before she suggested that Channel Seven might be willing to pay for at least part of the costs of a recovery operation. By this stage, using a recovery agency had been in my thoughts, but I hadn't given it serious consideration because it was out of my financial reach. The journalist's suggestion both stunned me and lifted my hopes. In the space of a mere sentence from someone I'd never met in person, I suddenly felt I was in a different world. The journalist said she would speak with Channel Seven and give me a definite answer as soon as she could.

Meanwhile, on Christmas Day I had more reason than ever to want my children back: I received an email from Ali. I hadn't heard from him for months, and then, unexpectedly, a message came through in which Ali wished me a 'Merry Christmas from us'. He said Lahela and Noah didn't hate me, and he never said anything bad about me to them. He also wrote that I would see the kids 'one day soon'.

Ali attached photos of Lahela and Noah, all of which I had already seen from friends via Ali's Facebook page. I felt that there was no sincere meaning behind sending them, it was just typical Ali playing emotional games with me. But I wasn't going to hit back. Finally I was over him and his tricks. Completely over him. I just wanted to physically hold my kids.

Two weeks later, on 8 January 2016, Lahela and Noah had a baby brother to love from afar. If only they knew. The birth, again at Royal Brisbane and Women's Hospital, had no complications. Little Eli was plump, fair and a bundle of contentment right from the start. And his father was in a happy state of pure wonderment. His whole family was, especially Barb; after Brendan had first rung and told her I was pregnant, she'd run outside her house, stood on the front lawn and yelled: 'I'm going to be a grandmother!' to all the neighbours. Seeing her tears of happiness when she held Eli, I imagined another similar announcement would be made when she got home.

Emotions were bubbling in the room when my phone rang. From memory, Eli was on my chest and his umbilical cord had just been cut. It was that quiet, bonding time with a new baby. Mum alerted me to the phone.

'It's all right, Mum, I'll look later.' She went over to turn it off.

'Well, this one looks like it's important because you've had a few missed calls from the same number.'

That made me react because I was expecting to hear about Channel Seven's decision any day. I answered before the phone rang out. It was the journalist calling with great news: Channel Seven was apparently going to fund the recovery operation.

I lost it immediately. Tears. The works.

'Oh my God!'

The journalist spoke with me briefly before saying she would give me some time to digest what she'd said. She didn't know I'd just had a baby, and I didn't tell her. We hung up, and Mum immediately asked what had happened. I told her, and Brendan's mum was there too. Here we all were, already crying because of baby Eli, and then the apparent support from Channel Seven set us off even more. Brendan's brother, Shane, walked into the room to find a bawling huddle of us. And all the while Brendan, bless him, just hugged and hugged me.

'This is the best day ever,' he said.

It was certainly the craziest hour I'd ever known, and it rounded out a mad bout of coincidence too. Eight months earlier, in the space of just four days, Ali dropped the bombshell that Lahela and Noah weren't coming home, and I found out I was pregnant; now, sitting in a birthing suite, I was celebrating the arrival of a new baby, and news that Lahela and Noah could be coming home after all. Someone was smiling on me, somewhere.

I went home nine hours after Eli was born; there was too much to do to stay in hospital. The journalist told me that Channel Seven wanted to use Child Abduction Recovery International (CARI), which was operated by Adam Whittington. I knew of Adam because I'd previously contacted him when I was examining all my options much earlier.

However, two or three days after Eli's birth, just as I was starting to get my head around what could possibly happen, I received another call.

'I'm so sorry, Sally.'

The words hit hard, and I knew straightaway what was coming: the journalist told me Channel Seven had decided to pull out of the story. The journalist appeared upset, but that didn't soften my anger towards her.

'So, that's it, then, is it?'

She acknowledged it was as far as Channel Seven was concerned, but she offered what I thought was only very slight hope when she said she had a friend at Channel Nine who worked at *60 Minutes*. Perhaps she could contact him to gauge interest? By no means was I going to stop her. Yes, it was worth a go. On that note, we hung up, and I held onto Eli and bawled. Brendan heard me and came into our bedroom.

'What's up?'

I threw my phone on the bed.

'They're not doing it!'

I know life is full of emotional upheavals that make human beings what we are, but at that point I would have given anything to be a bland so-and-so who didn't react to a thing. Emotions brought too much pain. I didn't know how much more hurt I could take. And all of this was dragging my thoughts away from Eli and the joy of a newborn.

However, in just a matter of hours I had changed my mind after I received another phone call.

'Sally Faulkner?'

'Yes.'

'This is Stephen Rice. I'm a producer from *60 Minutes*.'

Chapter Seventeen

I needed to know quickly what Stephen Rice thought. If I was going to be disappointed again, I wanted to know that straightaway. He said he was interested to know more about my story. I told him everything, while hinting that Channel Seven was also considering doing something and I needed a swift yes or no. Stephen, who seemed a really lovely guy, accepted that but I still felt strange about bluffing him. The next morning he rang to say *60 Minutes* was very interested, and would pay for the whole recovery. As had become so very normal, I began to cry. I apologised for being emotional and perhaps making Stephen feel awkward, but he told me my reaction was understandable. It was a reasonably short conversation, and he assured me he would be in contact again soon.

That phone call started a long process of emails between me, Stephen and Adam Whittington from CARI, which was the company *60 Minutes,* like *Sunday Night,* chose to involve. Stephen asked me what I knew about Adam. I told him I'd done some previous research and discovered that Adam was an ex-soldier, and that CARI was more expensive than some of the other agencies I'd looked at. I assumed CARI had been automatically passed down from the Channel Seven proposal, and I didn't feel I was in a position to question anything. I didn't ask about that.

The reality of what was happening really hit home when Adam arranged to meet me, along with Mum, Brendan and Eli, at a Brisbane coffee shop in February. It turned into quite a marathon, lasting a few hours. I asked most of the questions, and Adam did most of the talking, though I did fill him in on Ali and his family. I mentioned that they had political connections – but that my Lebanese lawyer had told me it wasn't relevant to this situation. No recovery specifics were discussed. I think he was sussing me out.

I liked Adam. Of all the things I had expected him to tell us, there was one moment of complete surprise when he pulled out his phone and said: 'I actually have photos of your children.' He had taken them on a previous trip to Lebanon after I had initially contacted him with a general enquiry about child recovery. He was obviously prepared for a follow-up that never came from me.

I was stunned, and at first I didn't quite believe the pictures could be real. Lahela and Noah had both grown. Through my tears, I looked at them playing with a black cat near Ali's surf shop. Lahela loved animals, and had all too briefly grown up with cats, chickens and ducks at my mum's place. I couldn't know if the cat in the picture was a pet or one that lived at the beach.

'How did they look to you?' I asked Adam.

He told me they appeared well looked after, but they didn't seem happy. That was like a knife through my heart. He told me that in the hour he watched them he didn't see them smile; he did, however, see them run round as normal kids would be expected to do, but, he stressed, there was no animation. I burst into tears.

Adam told me that that sort of behaviour was typical for many abducted children who were taken from a familiar environment and forced to start again in a strange place with a markedly different culture. This was no surprise to me, but it was only when hearing it from a person who had observed my children first-hand that the full gravity of the situation struck me. I felt sick for the rest of our meeting.

Once it was over, I walked away with no doubt that Ali had done the wrong thing, and I had every right to try to recover the children. I wanted to bring home my children as soon as I could. And, after all the uncertainty of the previous months, it was now a true possibility. When I had asked Adam about the likelihood of a successful recovery, he lit up my world when he said he didn't take on a job unless he thought it could be pulled off. For the first time since that horrible day on 22 May 2015 I thought: *My God, this is really going to happen.*

Over the following weeks the emails continued. I didn't question any of it. I didn't care what I had to do, how many interviews they needed or who paid whom, as long as someone was helping me bring Lahela and Noah home.

At some point, there was a lull in communications for about a week. I wasn't worried because I assumed we were waiting for everything to be organised. This, after all, was no small operation. Finally, I received a group email with a few stipulations. I also received a phone call from Stephen saying that it was likely Tara Brown would be the reporter covering the story and that he wanted to arrange the first in-depth interview. I told him I wasn't comfortable filming an interview at my mum's house. Stephen accepted this, and the interview was arranged at Brisbane's Stamford Plaza hotel.

I arrived in the morning with Dana and Sacha, who had offered to babysit Eli during what Stephen had told me would be a long and often intense process. We met Stephen in the hotel foyer, and he was initially confused about which of the three blonde women was actually me. It was the first time I'd met him in person, but I already knew what he looked like thanks to Google. He was middle-aged, bald and bearded, and had a serious manner.

Soon afterwards we were up in the hotel's penthouse suite meeting Tara. She was immaculately made-up. I remember glancing at Sacha, who was wide-eyed and star-struck, while Dana played it cool; she was always the poker-face girl. I felt very intimidated as I shook Tara's hand and she gave me a warm smile. This was so far from anything I had ever thought would happen to me. But now, I was about to sit down opposite one of Australia's most recognised journalists, a household name. It may sound a weird thing to say, but as I looked at Tara, I found it hard to believe she was actually human. She was beautiful and seemed perfect, all so stiff and proper, with not a hair out of place. She said she would like to get to know me on a personal level, but I thought to myself, *There's no way that's ever going to happen, because we don't have anything in common.* How was I to know how much my views would change in the weeks ahead?

Before we sat down for the interview, Stephen asked me if I'd had any recent contact from Ali. No. Tara also asked a few questions, and she seemed particularly interested to know if I thought Ali would have any suspicions at all about what was happening. My answer was double-pronged: Ali wouldn't know I would have the finances to arrange a recovery, nor would he ever think I would have the courage to try one. He didn't realise that my love for Lahela and

Noah had made me steel myself to fight this hard for my children. So, I could only say that he had no inkling at all. I could tell that Stephen was very wary and was assessing my answers and body language, which made me even more nervous. He then said the interview would start in about fifteen minutes. I went and breastfed Eli in a huge bedroom with an adjoining spa that overlooked the Brisbane river. In a very different mood to the one in the interview area, Sacha and Dana were joking around and taking selfies with Eli in the spa. They helped me relax, but as soon as I walked back out into a glare of lights and strange faces, I tensed up again. Stephen introduced me to the cameraman, Ben Williamson, and I think his sound operator, David Ballment, was also there, but I'm not sure. I was incredibly nervous and trying not to show it. There were others present too, but again I can't recall them exactly; I was too flustered by what was about to happen to take everything in.

Tara was already seated, and she invited me to sit down opposite her.

'Just try to relax,' she said.

Does that ever work? It only made me tense up more. A guy who was working with the lighting asked me to move a little bit one way and then the other. I did that while looking at Tara, who had a half-smile on her face; every time I looked away from her, the smile stopped, and then when I looked back again, it started. I became even more nervous.

Finally, we began the interview, and Tara talked me through each question before she asked it properly. I kept thinking: *I'm on* 60 Minutes*! Is this real?* The questions were all as I had expected: 'When did Ali take Lahela and Noah?' 'How did you feel?' 'What have you been doing since you lost your children?' Occasionally Tara would stop me after an answer and ask me if there was anything else I would like to add. We'd then do the question, or one similar to it, all over again. Meanwhile, Stephen sat listening intensely on a chair to the side of us. Most of the time he had his legs crossed, and his chin rested in one hand. Again, I could tell he was summing up everything I said. Whenever I glanced across at him, he seemed very much in the zone. To me, an outsider with no experience of anything like this, the strangest part of the whole process was when Tara asked questions that were purely for the sake of the camera. I didn't have to reply; I just looked at her asking these questions that I'd already heard. It was all so strange, and by the end of the interview, I was barely able to look at anyone.

The interview process took a few hours, after which Stephen sounded me out about speaking with some of my family. After being guided through the hardest part by Tara, I felt comfortable enough to ring Mum and ask if we could all go to her place. Mum was fine with everything. My brother Simon was also there, and it was during his interview that I understood for the first time how deeply he'd been affected by the loss of Lahela and Noah. Simon, like my dad, does not show emotions easily, but as he told his story to Tara, the tears started to flow. He recalled the day he was at work when a colleague asked him what was happening with his niece and nephew. Until then, Simon had been very restrained about the issue, but for whatever reason that question at that time was enough to snap him, and he fell apart. Just lost it. His workmate apologised, but Simon was inconsolable. His boss gave him some time off; I knew he was away from work, but he hadn't told me the real reason, only that he didn't feel well. Now, listening to him open his heart to *60 Minutes*, I felt gutted for him. We both cried.

While we were filming, I received a video message. It was great timing for *60 Minutes*, because the video showed surveillance footage of Lahela and Noah being walked to school by Ali's mother. It seemed so surreal that I wondered for a moment if I could reach through the screen and touch them. I was pretty emotional, and the *60 Minutes* guys filmed a sequence of me watching the video. It was just greater confirmation that I was in the middle of a very real situation. Yet, I still had trouble grasping the reality; it seemed like I was having an out-of-body experience where I was looking down at myself playing the role in a movie or on the stage. I would never have thought in a million years that I would be forced to these lengths to see my children.

The filming lasted all day, and the next morning Ben took some shots of me in a local park and playground. Then, we all went our own ways. I assumed the *60 Minutes* crew would roll on to other stories, and return to thinking about mine when the time came. But for me? Well, it was difficult not to think about anything else. I tried to stay calm and forced myself to focus on Eli and Brendan. That only partially worked. I had begun the countdown to seeing Lahela and Noah again. I was daring to believe this was going to happen.

Part III

Me as a baby with Mum and Dad (*top left*). Despite my mum and dad's marriage breakdown I had a safe, loving childhood. I was an animal-loving, outdoors girl who barely watched TV; I even won the occasional medal for figure-skating on rollerskates. I was very proud of my daggy old leotard!

When I was 21 I saw an advertisement for a job with Emirates. I felt like I'd won the jackpot when I was offered a position as a flight attendant. One day I was finishing my uni degree, the next I was off to see the world.

A phone call in July 2008 changed my life and took me to the party where I met Ali Elamine. Charming, handsome, funny – I fell in love with Ali and his Californian accent.

I didn't realise how much love I had to give until my daughter came along. Ali was besotted immediately. Lahela and me on my wedding day (*below right*).

Me and Ali sealing our marriage with a kiss.

Showing off Lahela on our wedding day.

Me and my girl (*top*). I thought moving to Beirut to support Ali's new job would bring us together, but the cracks began to show not long after we arrived. I was in denial but when he first took Lahela from me I broke.

When we visited Ali's family in Chakra we stayed at their home (*top*). I loved the countryside and only wish I could have felt more at ease.

Me with Lahela. I told myself that things would get better and I was prepared to fight for my marriage. If that meant returning to Beirut, then that's what I'd do.

Chapter Eighteen

The country did not matter. If Lahela and Noah were in Germany, England, the United States, or any other place on the planet, I would have gone there to get them if all other avenues to retrieve them had failed. I wanted my children back. That was it. They had been deceitfully taken from me, and it was time to right a wrong. The fact that I had to do this in a country so culturally different to my own was not an indication that I disrespected that country. It was simply confirmation that my love for my children overrode everything else. I ask any parent who loves their kids what they would do in a similar circumstance. Certainly, there will be different answers, but for me, there was only one. I would give my life for any of my three children. If that meant standing in front of a killer with a gun, I would do it. If that meant giving my heart or another organ, I would do it. I say again, I wanted my children back. Yet, if I got them back, I had already decided that Ali would still be able to come to Australia to visit them. Yes, I resented so many things he'd done, but I was determined that my feelings towards him would not spill over to affect his relationship with our children. We were both parents, and we both had a duty to provide the very best for Lahela and Noah. I knew better than most the agony of being denied access to your children.

Ali's behaviour told me he really didn't give a damn about them, but I did. They loved their dad and I would never do to him what he had done to me. I would never deny him access or stop him from talking to them. It had been almost ten months since I'd spoken to the children – too long. Yes, I was going to bring them home, but I didn't see that as kidnapping or hurting Ali, I was just righting his wrong.

And that's the way I felt when I arrived in Beirut on Saturday, 2 April 2016. I had bought my own ticket and flown out separately to the *60 Minutes* crew; it was suggested that I shouldn't stay in the same hotel as the TV guys. I was told I would hear more about the plans on the Saturday evening. At that stage I did not know about specifics.

To tell my story I need to include details of what happened in Beirut but I am also aware that anything I say about the recovery in this book could be used against me or others. I also signed a contract with the recovery agency that required confidentiality and I can't go against this as I have recently been notified by the agency that I will be sued if I do. However, many of the details of the recovery that have already been revealed can be discussed as I am not divulging anything not already known. For this reason, there are some details I won't disclose, but the emotions will all be revealed. I know others have judged me, along with the *60 Minutes* team and Adam Whittington, but I won't say a bad word about any of them because they helped me when no one else would.

I contacted Stephen and we arranged to meet at the Phoenicia Hotel, where the *60 Minutes* crew were staying, on Sunday morning. By then, we expected to have a more thorough understanding of what lay ahead over the following days. However, Saturday went by without any news from Adam. I was panicked and immediately thought he was a no-show. But I tried to convince myself that he must have been held up by some unexpected mishap. It was, however, very unsettling, and I spent an anxious night in my hotel room knowing my children were so close and I couldn't rush to them.

The next morning I went to the Phoenicia, where I found Stephen waiting for me in the restaurant. He didn't recognise me at first because I was wearing a turquoise-and-blue patterned headscarf; I felt a bit silly in it, but it was the best way to hide my blonde hair whenever I was in public view. We were only fifteen minutes' drive away from Ali's apartment, and the thought had crossed my mind that I could be spotted by Ali or one of his friends. As a result, I soon got into the habit of looking down at the ground to further hide my face.

Stephen ordered me a coffee and we chatted as we waited for Adam. We were both concerned that we still hadn't heard from him. Time was ticking by, especially considering the recovery attempt was expected to happen as soon as the next day. The cameraman, Ben Williamson, arrived a while later. He had been out looking around the streets, and was ready to take me out to film some background footage. I liked Ben right from the beginning. He was a really friendly, thoughtful guy who tried his best to make me feel comfortable. At one stage we sat down at a restaurant to film with a small camera, and we started to chat about his two young daughters. Afterwards, he dropped me back in the *60 Minutes* hire car to my hotel, which was a lot more downmarket than theirs.

Again, all I could do was wait. I Skype-called Mum to tell her what was going on. She was worried. In the afternoon, I messaged Stephen, who replied straightaway. Thank goodness. There'd been news. Relief flooded through me, and I forced myself to sit down, even if I couldn't truly relax.

Now, I hoped there would be no further distractions; simply waiting was challenging enough.

When I finally saw Adam I asked him how confident he was I would be reunited with Lahela and Noah, and I remember his answer clearly: 'Almost a hundred per cent.' He acknowledged the only problem he'd ever had in a recovery was in Singapore when he was arrested and sentenced to sixteen weeks' jail; he explained the incident and blamed its failure on false information given to him.

'I haven't told you any lies,' I promised.

'I've no doubt about that. I believe you.'

The next day, Monday, there was some uncertainty over whether or not it was a school holiday. Everyone involved in the recovery prepared as though this was going to be the big day, but it was indeed a holiday, so it was back to waiting.

I went with the *60 Minutes* crew to a boat at a marina. It made me uneasy because here was a television crew with a beautiful Anglo female presenter piling onto a cruiser-style vessel while other boats passed by, coming and going. If ever there was a way to draw attention to ourselves, this was it. I was terrified that word would get to Ali that I was in Lebanon. Ben filmed Tara, Adam and me sitting around a table below deck looking at a map. The curtains were drawn, and the windows and door were shut. It was very hot.

Later that day I moved to a better hotel, close to where the *60 Minutes* crew were now staying at the Mövenpick.

I went to bed feeling sick and edgy. And that feeling only became worse the next morning after the recovery attempt was aborted. The reason: Ali was seen taking Noah and Lahela to school. It had already been decided that any recovery would only be attempted when Ali's mother was the children's escort. None of us knew how Ali would react, and I didn't want Lahela and Noah to face any more distress than absolutely necessary. Seeing their mum and dad screaming at each other wouldn't be good.

I was glad the recovery had been stopped before I had a chance to see Lahela and Noah, because I doubt I would have been able to contain myself if I'd actually caught a glimpse of them. I was becoming more and more anxious. After another debrief I went back to my hotel and, after talking to Brendan, I spent most of the day in bed. The hours crept by. Night-time was even slower. I barely slept.

Early the next morning, Wednesday, 6 April, I got up, dressed and left the hotel to meet up with the team at a designated spot close by. It was déjà vu, but the mood seemed more tense and frantic than it had been the previous two days. David Ballment, the *60 Minutes* sound operator, put a microphone on me, while Ben was busy preparing his camera equipment. I think he filmed me, but I'm not sure. There was some concern over where GoPros would be placed in the vehicle, because we would have to pass through a checkpoint and didn't want anything to look unusual. Thankfully, we had a bigger car this day. It was a silver Hyundai sedan. Ben and I got into it with the recovery team at about 6am. The streets were still relatively quiet, but within another hour they would become a lot busier.

We drove for about twenty minutes and were in position around the corner from the school road before 7am. The familiarity of the area haunted me. The apartment in which I'd had so many horrible moments was just a few minutes' walk away. I held my hand to my headscarf and kept my head down as much as I could. Ben, who was sitting in the front, turned to me.

'Are you okay?' he asked.

'I don't feel very well.'

'Yeah, I'm feeling a bit nervous about the whole thing.'

We waited.

And waited.

It seemed like a year passed.

I kept looking over my shoulder to see if Lahela and Noah were on their way. I also looked at Ben, and the driver. The men either side of me in the back didn't say much, but the words that were spoken were a confusion of English and Arabic. I felt my heart race, and my whole body shook.

A phone rang. The driver answered it, then nodded and turned to me. It was time to move. Ali's mother and her maid had the children.

It was going to happen. It was really going to happen.

The men next to me told me to calm down. I tried to, but how could I?

Ben shifted in his seat. 'Fuck, fuck,' he said under his breath.

I was trembling.

Goose-bumps.

Clenched fists.

I was going to see my children.

Chapter Nineteen

I had them back.

Ten-and-a-half months of pain and anguish were over.

I was so happy to hold them. I felt no relief, though. We weren't home yet.

My arms were still tired after carrying Lahela and Noah up a few flights of stairs and through a maze of small, dark laneways riddled with bunches of exposed electrical wires and a sickening stench of garbage. We made it to an apartment, a small, crowded space with a living room and one bedroom that contained two single beds, a chest of drawers and other bits of furniture. There was also a bathroom and a kitchen with a small window that looked out onto multi-floored concrete buildings and windows, many of which had laundry hanging from them. I had never been to this part of Beirut, and from what I'd seen on the drive it had to be one of the poorer parts of the city; a considerable number of the buildings were pockmarked or shelled out. Many weeks later I would find out the area was Sabra, which was very much a needful place. Now, at 8am on Wednesday, 6 April 2016, it was the temporary home for Lahela, Noah and me. We'd made it to the safe house.

The previous hour had been the biggest adrenaline rush of my life. And, still shaking, I was hoping I would never, ever have to feel the same rush again. The recovery had all happened in a blink. One moment Lahela and Noah had been walking with Ali's mum and her maid on the side of the road, then the next the children were in the car crying hysterically while I tried to calm them down.

'It's Mummy. It's Mummy. Lahela. Noah. It's your mummy. It's all right.'

It felt as though I said that a thousand times in a matter of seconds. Lahela finally took a breath and looked at me sitting next to her. She did a double-take and immediately stopped crying.

'Noah, look it's Mummy. She came to get us. It's Mummy.'

She was clutching a schoolbag. She twisted it behind her, and reached out to me.

'Mummy!' she said as we hugged. 'I missed you.'

'I missed you guys too. Mummy loves you. I haven't forgotten about you. Mummy has come to take you home.'

'Good. We want to go back to Australia.'

Noah was still teary and looked confused; it was obvious he didn't understand what was going on. I couldn't say exactly how I felt either.

We were told by someone in the car to squish down as much as we could. Lahela leaned back on me until her head was just above the windowsill. Noah, who had been sitting between two of the recovery men, was moved next to me on my right. He kept looking at me, confused and uncertain. Meanwhile, Lahela began to chat about her day, and asked if a window could be wound down because she was getting hot. It couldn't. Lahela didn't miss a beat and just kept on talking, seemingly oblivious to what was happening.

As we drove away, it wasn't long before we heard police cars with sirens screaming through the streets, but thankfully they were heading away from us. That put me highly on edge, but I was determined not to show any of my fears to my children; I had to behave as normally as possible.

My nerves worsened when we pulled up behind a truck in which about twenty police officers, all with guns, sat in rows. The truck had no back door, meaning there was little more than a few metres and the thickness of a windscreen between us. I was sure the officers were looking straight at us. Our driver lit a cigarette, rolled down his window and pretended this happened to him every day. He seemed so cool. By then, Lahela and Noah were quite calm. But how could I be, with all these official eyes staring at us minute after minute?

'Do we have to follow them?' I asked.

One of the recovery men said we had no choice but to keep following the truck because we had to go along a route that had no checkpoints. We must have been behind the truck for ten, maybe twenty minutes. My heart was in my throat, while all the time I was still trying to give the impression to my children there was nothing at all to worry about.

'Noah, do you remember Mummy?'

'Uh-huh.'

I thought it was best not to push him, but then Lahela started to ask him the same question and told me that she and Noah looked at pictures of me on their iPad every day. In the light of the circus craziness going on around us, that moment helped settle me. The physical ache in my heart that I had stopped even noticing disappeared for the first time in ten months. I was overjoyed to see that I hadn't been forgotten.

We pulled onto a freeway, and then – thank God – the police truck went along another road. Throughout the car trip Ben filmed as much as he could. He asked me a few questions for the camera. He looked happy for the children and me, but I felt his bigger thought was one that was also consuming me: let's get this over with as soon as possible.

I don't know for how long we drove. Time was irrelevant. Safety and secrecy were all that mattered. We arrived at the safe-house apartment block and parked in a space that was about the size of a small garage, with buildings jammed all around it. I felt very uneasy about where we were going, and I was only just a little more comfortable after we were inside the safe house and the front door was shut.

A man and a woman lived in the apartment we were going to stay in, and I was introduced to them by their son, Mohammed, who had been part of the recovery team. Now, here we were, four strangers – a mother, two children and a cameraman – who had swept into a family's life to hide and wait. If all went well, we would stay only for a couple of hours before going on our way.

In the meantime, I settled down and did what I hadn't been able to do for all too long: I played with Lahela and Noah. They had both changed in so many ways. Noah had lost his chubbiness and was looking like a proper little boy, while Lahela, with those inquisitive brown eyes, was so much prettier, and in some inexplicable way she also looked wiser. Maybe my reasoning was influenced by her behaviour as she played with alphabet fridge magnets, spelling out words that I would never have managed when I was five. She also proudly showed me her report card that was in her schoolbag. Straight As.

'I'm so proud of you, Lahela.'

Her face lit up. 'Mummy, can I sing you a song?'

'Yes, sweetie.'

'It's a Mother's Day song.'

Such a beautiful soft voice. I cuddled her and put my nose against her hair and took a deep breath.

I gave Noah two wooden pull-back toy cars and some sticker books that I'd brought from Australia. He was happy, and in the way that little boys with toys can be, he was in a world of his own. I also had a surprise for Lahela, and pulled out from my bag *The Pout-Pout Fish*.

'Remember this?' I asked.

To me, it was much more than a storybook; it was a key to our past. And to feel my daughter snuggle up next to me in this strange environment and go to our happy place warmed my heart. Yet I was still very much on edge, and I doubted anything would change that until we were out of the country and heading for home.

We'd only been at the safe house for about half an hour when Adam turned up with Tara and Stephen, and David the sound operator whom I'd come to know by his nickname, Tangles. Tara, as usual, looked immaculate, which reminded me of what I'd thought when we'd done the interview on the boat two days earlier: there wasn't anything more likely to draw attention than an elegant blonde Anglo woman dressed in a pinkish work suit walking through a dingy Arabic rabbit warren with three Anglo men.

'I wouldn't ever be able to find this place again in a million years,' said Tara before asking, 'How do you feel, Sally?'

'I'm so stressed. That was really intense. Lahela and Noah cried. I hated that.' I hated that for those few minutes Lahela and Noah had been frightened and hadn't known what was happening. Until they saw my face they were scared. I had to live with that.

While I spoke to Tara, I heard Stephen and the crew talking in the background about whether or not I was still wearing a microphone. I was. Almost immediately, Tara asked me if we could do an interview. She was very sincere with her request, but I was like a piece of wire that was being screwed tighter and tighter. If we didn't get out of the safe house soon, I knew I was in danger of snapping. The last thing I felt capable of was an interview. However, I knew Tara and the crew were only doing their job, and the interview was the reason they'd helped me in the first place. I owed them a lot because they'd reunited me with Lahela and Noah.

We did a brief interview with the expected 'How do you feel?' type questions, and Ben filmed the children playing. Then Adam, who was yet to tell us of our exit plan, said to me: 'You should make that call now.' This was a strategy that I'd been struggling to come to terms with ever since Adam had told me that after any recovery operation it was usual procedure for the parent of the recovered child or children to contact their former partner and assure them that the children were safe and well. I accepted that, but I thought it made sense for such contact to be made *after* we'd left the country. However, Adam assured me that all would be fine. This was obviously a film-worthy moment for *60 Minutes*, and Stephen asked Ben and Tangles to prepare. I was very worried about the effect the sound of Ali's voice might have on the children, and Stephen understood my concern and decided the phone call would be filmed, but not with Ali on speaker.

So, I made the call.

Ali answered immediately: 'Sal.'

His response alarmed me. He sounded so composed and familiar, and the way he said my name gave me chills. I was ringing from a Lebanese number; how on earth could Ali have known it was me? My thoughts flashed back to the recovery, where, for just a moment, Ali's mother and I had caught sight of each other. The look in her eyes was, to me, one of pure hatred. She knew I was there and would have told Ali.

I continued. 'Ali?'

'Yep.'

'I'm just letting you know the kids are okay.'

'Yep.'

'They are with me and they're safe.'

'Uh-huh.'

I couldn't get anything out of him. No long words. No emotion. If the roles had been reversed, I know I would have been hysterical. But Ali was calm – weirdly calm – which made me feel even more uncomfortable. Adam encouraged me to keep talking. He'd told me what to say. 'If you want to see the kids before I go, meet me at the Australian embassy at nine o'clock on Monday morning.'

'So, you're at the embassy?'

'I'm not telling you where I am, but if you want to say goodbye to the kids, meet me at the Australian embassy at nine on Monday.'

'Yep, we'll see.'

He hung up.

A few minutes later, I received a message from him on WhatsApp. He had blocked me from his account for months, but now he said he wanted further reassurance about the kids, and requested that I take a photo of Lahela and Noah and send it to him. There was no way I was going to do that because he might have been able to discover where we were, so I replied, 'No.' Ali then asked for a voice recording of the children. Again, 'No.' I wrote that I was willing to talk with him, but that was it, nothing more. He replied, 'All right, no worries.' And that was the end of our exchange.

I was still shaken by Ali's actions when Adam announced he was going to make final preparations. He told me we would leave the safe house in two to three hours.

'I'll call you in an hour,' he said. 'But if you don't hear from me, don't call me.'

After he left we set up for a longer interview. Of all the questions Tara asked, there was only one I wasn't prepared for. What happened if I was caught? That rattled me. I can't remember my exact answer, but I'm pretty sure I replied in a way that implied we'd all be screwed. It was the one question I didn't want to think about.

But soon enough, I had no choice. In fact, none of us did.

'Look, look,' said the woman who lived in the apartment.

We all turned towards the television in the lounge room to see Ali on the screen making some sort of media state-ment. Lahela caught a glimpse of him, but she and Noah were quickly ushered into the bedroom by Tara, who used a gigantic teddy bear as a distraction. As the kids started to jump over the bear, I listened to Ali speak in Arabic in a very serious tone but with a half-smile on his face, which seemed odd to me. Mohammed translated.

'Four armed men have taken my children.'

The mood in the lounge room changed instantly. I looked across and saw Stephen deflate in his chair. He turned pale, almost white. I wanted to throw up.

Ali's mother then appeared on screen and said that she'd been hit on the head by at least one of the men, and had been pushed to the ground. She added she didn't know who now had her grandchildren. Lies. I had seen her during the recovery: she tripped; and she damn well knew who had Lahela and Noah. And as for Ali and his accusation of four armed men? There were only three men as one had left the car earlier to scout ahead, and none of them was carrying a gun. I would never have agreed to any guns near my kids. But Ali and his mother seemed to me to be playing on public emotion to gain as much support in as short a space of time as possible. Ali said nothing about the children being with their mother, despite knowing full well they were.

From then on, it seemed that whatever channel we switched to, Ali and his mother were there to remind us of our situation. I grew more and more anxious to hear from Adam. At least an hour had passed since he'd left us, but we'd had no word from him. Stephen kept his eyes on the news services, and after watching yet another report, he looked at me and shook his head. I had my own negative thoughts, but to see Stephen, a hardened journalist, respond in that way confirmed we were in serious trouble. Meanwhile, the kids were still happily playing.

'Would you like to speak with Nana?' I asked them.

Lahela responded enthusiastically. So, we called Mum on WhatsApp. Simon was with her at the time, which made the kids even happier, and gave me some strength. At the other end, I knew Mum and my brother would have been over the moon. I dared not tell them, though, of our predicament.

By midday, about four hours after the kids and I arrived at the safe house – and about three since Adam's departure – we still hadn't heard from the man in charge of getting us out. The lounge room was very quiet. Some people drifted in and out of light sleep, a tiny breeze blew through the kitchen window, and Tara's interview question banged about in my head: What happened if I was caught? Ali's face – and his mother's – flashed through my mind.

I was scared. More scared than I had ever been.

Chapter Twenty

Standing in the bathroom of the safe house, I had another reason to detest the man who had ignored our custody agreement, broken every promise he'd made and abducted our children. I had taken Noah to the toilet, which had no running water, and I discovered that he had recently been circumcised.

I stared at the area of redness and forced myself to hold back the tears. What was wrong with Ali? He had wanted Noah to be cut from the day he was born, but I saw no need. Ali and I had argued about it until Ali backed down; it had been resolved when Noah was a baby and had never been discussed since. But now? Noah wasn't yet three and a half. How could Ali have been allowed to have this done without both parents' approval? I was so angry; after all that

Ali had done, this was something I had never considered. My poor baby boy. And I hadn't been there to comfort him. How scared he must have been.

'Does it hurt, sweetie?'

'A little bit.'

A whole new wave of emotion and nausea swept over me. I felt rage building. What else? What else, Ali? His name alone made me furious.

I fought to remain calm so I didn't distress Noah as I walked back into the lounge room.

'Are you all right?' asked Stephen.

I didn't trust myself to say more than, 'Noah's been circumcised.'

'Oh, that's really confronting,' said Tara.

'Extremely.'

I don't think anyone really knew what to say.

We were all so flat and tired, and the kids were getting bored and hungry. Lahela started to speak in Arabic to me, but I couldn't understand a word. It was another marker of all the time and experiences I'd missed with her. She became the link between the westerners in the room and the woman whose home it was. I asked Lahela to become our translator and ask the woman if she could please help us get something to eat. Amid the tension of our situation, there was something so fragile yet powerful in seeing a five-year-old girl control the moment. I felt such pride in Lahela.

The woman was very obliging. We gave her money and she went out to buy sandwiches. The rest of us stayed in the apartment; our closest contact with the world beyond the front door was little more than the continuing breeze through the kitchen window, the incessant beeping of some type of machine or device somewhere close by, and the muffled sounds of voices on the streets.

After eating, Lahela and Noah snuggled up against me and fell asleep on the couch. Ben grabbed my phone and took some photos of us, and he also filmed us and the apartment. Stephen sat cross-legged on his chair, and Tara, on the couch as well, rested her head against one of her arms. All four of the *60 Minutes* crew dozed off at different times, and so did I. The adrenaline of the morning had worn off, and was replaced by fatigue and the draining acceptance of a sickening reality. I had my children with me, but how would I get us home? Occasionally, we were stirred by bellowing male voices in laneways and corridors. The first time I heard them I immediately thought: *The police!* and I took a deep breath and waited for a knock on the door. On one occasion I opened my eyes and looked around at every face. Everyone was asleep. It was quite peaceful, in a disturbing, calm-before-the-storm sort of way.

This went on for maybe two hours, but I couldn't be sure because I had lost track of time. Then, the peace and quiet was abruptly shattered. The front door flung open and Mohammed rushed in and told us to turn on the television: a news bulletin was broadcasting CCTV footage of the recovery. Taken from above the street, it showed Lahela and Noah walking with the maid while Ali's mother was a step behind. In an instant, one of the recovery men stepped out of the car, quickly followed by two others. A moment later the kids were in the car and being driven away. Mohammed translated, saying the media was reporting the incident as an abduction. My heart sank. Thankfully the kids were still asleep and were none the wiser. However, the expression on the face of everyone else in the lounge room told me more than words. I saw Stephen and Tara look at each other. Stephen barely blinked; Tara screwed up her face. Both shook their head. I felt my eyes fill with tears. At that very moment, with resignation so heavy in everyone's mind, I had an unexpected thought: I had to cherish this time, because my children and I were together. And who knew how long that would last?

The electricity soon cut out – it ran in roughly three-hour cycles – and the TV turned off. It was mid to late afternoon, and Stephen announced he would go back to the hotel in the early evening to see if he could work out what was going on. He left at about six o'clock, telling the rest of the *60 Minutes* crew to stay put and not to try to contact him, but if they didn't hear from him by nine o'clock they too were to make their way back to their hotel.

Time passed even more slowly. We sat on the lounge-room couch and exchanged looks more than words. No news came from Stephen, and by then we had all accepted that something unexpected had happened. Nearing nine o'clock, Tara announced the inevitable: she, Ben and Tangles would soon leave. Ben, not wanting to risk his footage and equipment, decided to leave all his gear at the apartment. He tried to reassure me.

'Hopefully we'll see you later tonight or tomorrow when all this is sorted.'

I don't know whether or not he believed what he was saying, but I appreciated his attempt to remain upbeat.

I took Lahela and Noah off to wash them before bedtime. The process was very basic: a bucket of cold water mixed in with a saucepan's worth of warm water heated on the stove. Afterwards, it was into the bedroom for what would I hoped be a full night's sleep. But both were full of energy and jumped up and down on the mattress.

'Will you cuddle me, Mummy?' said Lahela. 'Daddy doesn't cuddle me to sleep.'

'Of course I'll cuddle you, sweetie.'

'When I cry out Daddy just leaves me.'

'I'm here, sweetie. I'm not going to let you cry.'

'Will you cuddle me too?' asked Noah.

'Of course, come here.'

Tara walked in to say goodbye.

'Sweet dreams, you two. Have a big sleep and hopefully we'll be off to Australia tomorrow,' she said.

'I have dreams all the time and they are bad,' replied Lahela.

Tara was touched. She was a mother too, and I imagined there was no place she would have rather been than at home tucking her two boys into bed. Instead, she was being a reporter, but more importantly at that moment she was a shoulder and a heart for Lahela and Noah. She hugged them both.

'I'll see you later, Sally, and we'll speak soon.'

I didn't know when I would see her or any of the *60 Minutes* crew again.

That night, I couldn't sleep. I watched the clock until midnight, hoping that Tara or Stephen would contact me. Finally, someone from *60 Minutes* did, but it wasn't who I expected. Executive Producer Kirsty Thomson called me on WhatsApp from Sydney. She was really worried because she'd seen the CCTV footage of the incident and hadn't been able to get in touch with any of the crew. She asked me if I knew where they were, and it alarmed us both when I said no. Kirsty then asked me if another reporter, Michael Usher, could conduct an interview with me a little later on Skype. I didn't feel as though I could refuse.

After Kirsty's call I knew that everything had come undone. I knew that if they could, Adam and the *60 Minutes* crew would have contacted me. The only reason they hadn't done so was that they had been arrested. I was worried for them all and terrified at what this would mean for me and the children. The early hours went by in a daze. I contacted Brendan, just to hear his voice and to make sure Eli was okay. At some point I tried an Australian government travellers' emergency hotline number and was put through to an office, presumably in Canberra. The man I spoke with told me I was better to contact the Australian embassy in Beirut, but it would only answer during office hours, beginning at 8am. I explained the whole story to him, and asked if there was any way I could make urgent contact, but he said it was a matter of hanging tight; he did, however, say he would send a message through to the embassy. I doubted there was anything the embassy could do, anyway, and I thought that if I tried to get in with the children, I would be arrested by Lebanese police at the gate.

I didn't know what to do or how to get out of Lebanon safely. I only knew that things were very serious. Kirsty Thomson stayed in contact with me through the night, and in between these calls I started to think about what I could do on my own. I contemplated trying to arrange a boat, but that was a lottery proposition. First, I had to get to a marina with the kids, and then find the appropriate person and negotiate. It wasn't realistic; I would have no idea of the calibre of person I was dealing with, and even if I found someone trustworthy, there was a much greater likelihood of me being detained before Lahela, Noah and I had a chance to leave the shore. I wouldn't risk it. So, what could I do? My head was filled with crazy thoughts, which weren't helped by the darkness. I couldn't turn a light on because everyone else was asleep. It was then that I decided to message the recovery agent Col Chapman. He'd always been helpful and informative in the past and though I was reluctant to contact him, I felt I had no choice because I knew it was game over. I got through to him and told him I was in trouble, and asked if there was any way out of the mess I was in. Would a boat be an option? The cost, about 80 000 euros, was beyond me; the only remote possibility I had of getting that type of money was from Channel Nine, and I doubted that would happen or if I could even ask. Nevertheless, Col suggested I should. It was reassuring just to be able to contact someone who dealt with problems like this often, someone I trusted, but our conversation didn't give me any new options and I felt more on my own than ever.

I spent the remaining hours of darkness sitting up in the bed and magnifying every single sound I heard. Any second I expected the police to come. At least, Lahela and Noah slept well. They looked so beautiful and peaceful. Innocent children. Nestled up either side of me they were my comfort. I love them so very much.

At some time around daybreak, I talked on Skype with Michael Usher. By then the kids were awake and jumping around without a care in the world. Later, when I returned to Australia, Michael told me how calm I appeared during that interview. That really surprised me, because by that stage I had given up trying to relax at all. I must have looked and sounded dreadful. I was still trying to hide my anxiety from Lahela and Noah, so perhaps I succeeded in putting on a brave face. I didn't feel brave at all. After the interview, Kirsty Thomson spoke with me yet again and said she was arranging to send a security contractor to the apartment to pick up the footage and camera equipment. This worried me because I didn't want anyone to know where the children and I were. Kirsty assured me the contractor was solely employed by Channel Nine and couldn't be compromised in any way. I still had my doubts, and these only grew after I spoke with Brendan again on WhatsApp. He was worried about me and was helpless so far away. He told me not to trust anyone, but I had to.

'Don't tell them where you are,' he warned.

But Kirsty had been adamant she and *60 Minutes* would stick by me. She promised: 'We will not leave you, Sally. We will do whatever we can to get you out.' She was very stressed, and had cried down the line. I trusted her.

Later, I Skype-called Mum. I tried not to let on that everything was, quite frankly, going to shit, but she knew things were precarious. Despite this, Mum tried to remain positive and was much calmer than I expected her to be. She just kept wanting to talk to Lahela and Noah.

After breakfast I played with the children. Noah was happy running amok with his cars, while Lahela turned to one of her sticker books. My heart filled when I saw her write *I love Mum* on the top of one page. But a few minutes later, after I had been distracted with Noah, I looked around to see Lahela had scratched the words out so hard that her soft-tip pen had made the paper soggy.

'Oh, baby girl, what did you colour out there?' I asked.

Lahela looked at me with her big brown eyes. Once upon a time I had only ever seen happiness in them, but now there was utter sadness.

'It said, "I love Mum", but I scratched it out because I don't see you anymore, so I can't love you anymore.'

Oh God. I felt so broken. I couldn't speak; the tears would have ambushed me. Instead, I picked up a pen and wrote over and over and over on the same page: 'Mummy loves Lahela . . . Mummy loves Lahela . . . Mummy loves Lahela.'

'What do those words say?' I asked.

Lahela offered a half-smile and told me.

I hugged her.

'Those words are so true. I haven't been able to see you because I haven't been allowed to. I promise I will try to make this better. I love you and Noah to the moon and back, and always will.'

It was impossible not to compare the moment against a year earlier when Lahela had been so blissfully happy whenever she was colouring in or doing any type of art or craft. What had Ali done to her? He was breaking our children, and it seemed there was not a single authority in either Australia or Lebanon that would stop that from happening.

While we were playing, I also revealed to Lahela that she had another baby brother, and I showed her pictures of Eli. She asked to see more, then abruptly ran off and returned with the giant teddy bear.

'Will we get to see him when we go back to Australia?'

'Of course. You'll be able to give him cuddles too.'

'Noah. Guess what? I have two brothers now.'

Noah looked at her, but he didn't seem bothered; jumping on beds was much more important to him.

By nine or ten o'clock – just over a day after we had arrived at the safe house – the kids were still calm enough, but I could see they were tired of being inside for so long. Noah was sick of his cars and didn't know what to do with all his energy. Lahela was also looking for new things to do; she'd had enough of the sticker books, practising writing and playing with fridge magnets. Even listening to me read *The Pout-Pout Fish* had worn thin. So, the two of them had resorted to wrestling, and I had to warn them a few times to be quiet because their laughter bounced off the walls, and I feared it could be heard easily in the laneways outside. Mohammed had fallen sleep on the couch and was snoring loudly. Earlier, I had considered possible escape alternatives, including getting a car to take the kids and me to Syria. I can't believe I thought about travelling to Syria – it just shows how scared and desperate I felt. I doubt I would have done it, but every time I looked at Lahela and Noah I was terrified that at any moment they would be taken from me again. I had to cling to any possible escape plan and any hope I could.

So, yet again it was all just a waiting game. But for what? Although I hadn't yet been told for sure, I knew the *60 Minutes* crew and Adam Whittington were in trouble; Kirsty's constant contact with me was a reminder of that. And with no word from Adam or any of his team, there was no one, apart from Mohammed, to whom I could immediately turn. I had to wait until 8am and try to contact the embassy.

The morning breeze through the kitchen window had arrived, and I allowed my thoughts to wander. Wouldn't it be good to be under blue Australian skies right now? That thought alone drew me straight back to reality. I tortured myself. We should have left yesterday. Why were we still here? How long could this go on?

'*Get out! Get out!*'

The words broke my thoughts. The kind woman who had brought us food was yelling, almost shrieking at me in a mix of English and Arabic. She waved her arms frantically, and pointed to the door.

Lahela and Noah jumped off the floor and ran to me.

'It's okay,' I told them.

'Get out!'

Both children began to cry.

'Ssh, it's all right. We're okay.'

'Get out!'

I didn't need to ask what was happening. She had seen something through the window that alarmed her. She pushed me towards the front door.

'Get out! Get out!'

I picked up Lahela and Noah, and ran outside into the hallway, startling an old woman who was kneeling on the ground in prayer. The space was so narrow that with a child on each hip I had to turn sideways to move. Lahela and Noah clung to me. I reached an opening to the left where a piece of wood sat across a door-frame. I pushed it out of the way and entered a room where another woman was praying. She looked up at me, and I immediately knew that she recognised us. She started to rattle off something in Arabic and tried to stop me coming in.

'*La! La! La! La!* [No! No! No! No!]'

I shook my head and forced my way past her. She kept shouting, but I ignored her and moved into a tiny bathroom – just a couple of square metres – and slammed the door shut behind me. I held onto the handle as the woman tried to open it, and she quickly gave up. I crouched against a corner and over a squat toilet. We all heard men hurrying through the laneways. They had to be police. The woman stopped talking; I assumed she was now worried that if the police found us, she would be accused of helping us. I took a deep breath.

The police were so loud. They reached the apartment where we had been staying, and started to rumble around, moving furniture, shouting.

I held Lahela and Noah so tightly that I felt as though we were one person.

'Ssh, I'm sorry, babies. We are just playing some hide and seek.'

'Are those men looking for us?' asked Lahela. 'Why?'

'It's all right, sweetie. They're not bad people. They just don't want you to go back to Australia, and Mummy doesn't want you to stay here.'

I was horrified that I was causing the children more distress. Lahela was quite calm, but Noah was trembling, crying, hysterical. Drips from a shower fell on us and made me feel dirty. I kept looking at my children. Noah looked back and rested his head on my shoulder, and suddenly, something clicked in me. No. Hiding my kids in a reeking corner of a stranger's home, hoping against hope that we wouldn't be found. But, then what? Continue hiding in another room? Run from one place to the next? With tears and trembles and worst of all, fear? No.

'It's all right, guys. We are going to see the police now. They are probably going to take you back to Daddy, but Daddy will let Mummy see you guys from now on.'

'No, Mummy!' protested Lahela.

'It's okay. The police officers are nice men. They won't hurt us. Hold onto Mummy. Mummy's going to carry you both out.'

Lahela was accepting. Noah was still shaking.

I walked out and saw the woman I had disturbed. She was sitting on a stool scowling at me.

'*Afwan* [Sorry],' I said.

She shook her head and tut-tutted me as I walked out.

The laneway was crowded with police. Ten, fifteen of them all swarming round the entrance to the apartment. Some wore grey uniforms and were armed, others were in plain clothes. One of them turned and saw me. He said something in Arabic, and all heads turned. All eyes were on us. There was dead silence for a moment, then I said: 'Don't touch me. Don't touch my children. Let me carry them out.'

I started to cry.

'*Yalla, yalla,* [Hurry, come here],' said one of the officers.

215

I walked over, and a few officers grabbed my arm.

'Don't touch me,' I said.

Another officer told them to let go, and they did.

'Where is your stuff in here? asked someone in English.

I went into the apartment and pointed at Lahela's schoolbag, a suitcase and two backpacks that held clothes and toys for the kids. The police had already gathered a big bag of Ben's camera equipment. Everything was packed up and carried out. I was then told to walk down the stairs to the bottom of the building. Officers crowded around me as I carried the children.

We reached an unmarked car on the street, where about another ten officers stood in seemingly scattered spots nearby. For a moment I actually fantasised they were all there to escort us to the airport where Lahela, Noah and I would be put straight on a plane heading for Australia. However, that moment passed in a breath.

We were put into the car and driven away. I didn't need to ask where we were going. Our driver beeped the horn continually, while sirens blared on the escort car in front of us. There were police at intersections blocking traffic and waving and shouting at people to get out of the way. It seemed that half of Beirut had been blocked off to ensure our easy passage. At times it was manic, especially when our driver yelled and threw his hands every which way.

'Can you stop yelling! You're upsetting my children.'

It was true. Lahela and Noah were really distressed, and were sweating in the new clothes I'd bought them. I held onto them, and tried my best to reassure them that everything was going to be all right.

'Are we still going back to Australia?' asked Lahela.

'I don't think so, sweetie.'

'But you said we were.'

'I know I did. I wish we were, but things have changed. I think they are taking us to the police station. Mummy is going to be asked a few questions, and maybe you will see Daddy.'

And maybe I would see him too. The thought of that made me very angry. But I was also deeply worried.

Chapter Twenty-one

The room was plain. A water cooler stood in one corner; a window overlooked a small bitumen car park that contained a number of both marked and unmarked vehicles; and a couch sat against a wall near the only door, which led out to the left where there was a lift. A handful of police officers stood talking casually to each other.

'Can you stop smoking, please? There are children here.'

The officers agreed to my request – it was probably more an angry demand – and put out their cigarettes. They then waited for a man, who I assumed was in charge, to take control. He was the only policeman in the room not in uniform. Dressed in trousers and a white collared shirt, he sat next to me to the side of a large wooden desk covered in messy stacks of paperwork. He leaned forward and looked at me. We were only about a metre apart.

'How are you?' he asked in English.

'How do you think? I came over here for my children, and then you guys come along.'

'We are doing our job.'

'Well, it's a terrible job. You know these children need a mother, don't you?'

I think he was surprised that I was aggressive towards him. I was a bit surprised in myself.

'Would you like to tell us what happened?' he asked.

'No. But I'd like to know if you're going to give the kids back to Ali.'

'Who's Ali?'

'You know exactly who he is.'

'I don't know what you're talking about.'

'Really? You don't know who these kids' father is, yet you've arrested me and brought me to a police station because of what I've apparently done?'

The detective – if that's what he was – gave me a wry smile and asked if I wanted a Nescafé. (As I would come to know, none of the police referred to a coffee as anything but a Nescafé.) I asked for water, and both the children and I were given some. Another officer walked in and lit up a cigarette. I protested, and the officer nodded and walked out.

Noah, who had been sitting on my lap with Lahela, complained that he was hot, and asked me if he could sit on the couch. The police allowed him to, and one officer gave him a mobile phone to play with. Lahela remained where she was; she sat quietly listening to the detective and some of the police as they chatted. I gathered she understood some of what was being said, but I didn't want to ask her for fear of repercussions. Instead, her actions were enough to tell me. She put her head on my shoulder and hugged me; it was as though she knew she would soon be taken away from me, and wanted to savour the precious time we had left together. Noah, on the other hand, just sat with a blank, bored look on his face. I wished I could have scooped them up and taken them back to Chipmunks and forgotten anything had ever happened. I felt such agony for both my children. The confusion must have been overwhelming for them. I felt so sad, and so guilty. I kept thinking back to the moment I could have prevented all this: the moment I agreed to let Ali bring the children back to Lebanon. If only I'd said no.

The detective resumed his questions – 'Where are you from?' 'Why have you come to Lebanon?' and so on – and I decided it was best to say little. I wasn't going to cooperate or admit anything.

He smiled and said something in Arabic to the officers in the room. They laughed.

'What's so funny?' I said angrily.

'Nothing, nothing.'

He told me the kids and I were going to be taken to another station, which made me wonder if we were at some sort of detective headquarters. Later, I found out the detectives called themselves the FBI, and this first place we were in was a special operations post.

'I don't want to go to another station, thank you. Can you please take us to the Australian embassy?'

The detective shook his head. 'Don't worry. You will be okay. You're their mother. Nothing will happen to you.'

I had little confidence in what he said, and I had none at all after four officers took my arms and led me away, with Lahela and Noah each holding one of my hands. Both stared up at me. I didn't want to imagine what they were thinking.

As we walked out of the room, I caught a glimpse of myself in the mirror in the lift. I looked like hell. My eyes were red and watery; seeing them made me realise how sore they were. They stung with extreme tiredness. My head throbbed. My whole body ached. I was so consumed by my pain that I didn't notice when a translator joined us. She got into a police car with us and two other officers. Without saying anything to me, she reached across me and offered Lahela and Noah some nuts.

'Please don't do that,' I said.

'Maybe they are hungry.'

'They are not eating your nuts, okay?'

I didn't care who I offended, although the woman didn't seem at all bothered; she continued to eat, and annoyed me more and more with each crunch. Every nerve in my body was stretched to breaking point.

The drive was about forty minutes in heavy traffic. The kids and I didn't say much, but the officers and the translator chatted away to each other. Towards the end of the trip we went up some windy streets on a hill. Then, there was no mistaking our destination: a peachy-white single-floor building with a handful of concrete steps leading up to the entrance.

There were cars, cameras and faces everywhere. People were jostling and shouting. And standing quietly among the crowd was Ali. My skin crept. He was there with his brother, Wissam, and his friend, Mustafa, and an instructor from his surf school. All of them were lined up out the front of the station as though they were spectators waiting for a parade to pass by. Ali, only metres away from me, caught my eye and then turned away from me and from the children. Every muscle in my body was tense. I was almost holding my breath waiting for his reaction.

Men in plain clothes opened the car door, and then officers picked up Lahela and Noah from the back seat.

'Mummy!'

'Mummy is just here. It's okay.'

I asked the officers if I could carry the children, but they refused and walked in front of me as I was escorted by officers either side of me. Lahela reached back towards me, and I put out my hand so we could touch each other. As we approached the building's steps, I looked over at Ali. What a surprise it was to see those big cold eyes of his, and I got the same predictable glare from Wissam as well. I squeezed Lahela's hand and went up the stairs while looking at Noah, whose worried face popped over the shoulder of the officer who was carrying him. By now, I knew that the children understood I was in serious trouble.

As soon as we were inside the station, Lahela and Noah were taken with the translator into a room, but I was stopped from following them.

'You can't do that! Let me see my kids.'

I snapped. Lost it. Completely lost it. I tried to get past the officers who were blocking my way. They pushed me back and said something in Arabic. I shoved them with everything I had. I felt so much rage that I suddenly didn't feel tired. The officers, the detectives, the translator, the whole miserable police station; Ali, his mother, his brothers, his friends; everyone was against me. I had to fight them all. I kicked out at the officers, I tried to push them away, I cried out.

'Give me my children back! I want to see my children!'

More officers came to restrain me. I didn't care; I was driven by the sight of my frightened children, and their fragile calls of, 'Mummy! Mummy! Mummy!'

I started to cry. 'Please, let me see my babies!'

But it was no use. I was handcuffed and manhandled away while Lahela and Noah kept screaming out for me.

'Please don't take my babies away from me,' I begged them. '*Please* don't take them again. I love them, they love me. Can't you hear what they're saying? They want their mum! Please! Please don't take them away again!'

I was almost hysterical but no one cared. I was pushed past a room where I glanced over to see the entire *60 Minutes* crew sitting slouched and handcuffed on a bed against a concrete wall. I felt a wave of dizziness as the confirmation hit home. I was right, everyone had been arrested. I wanted to stop and talk to the crew, but I was shunted away to a dark room with no windows. It was only a few square metres in size, and had no furniture. The door was shut behind me. I was alone. I couldn't hear the children. My eyes stung with tears.

I leaned up against a wall, stared at the floor and questioned my worth as a person and as a mother. Had I failed? Or was this the moment that made me realise how much fight I still had left in me? Either way, I realised I had come to a point in my life that was so far outside my normal existence that I was behaving in ways that made me question who I was, and who I might become. I was doing this all for my children. Everything was for them and I truly believed that I would give Lahela and Noah more love and a better life in Brisbane than they would ever know with Ali in Beirut, because they would know both parents. But at what cost? Was there a point at which I had to walk away and accept that I had to begin again? After all, I had a three-month-old baby and a partner who showed me loyalty and love. I owed it to them to give them all of me. Even as I was thinking this, I knew I could never stop fighting for Lahela and Noah. My God, I was hurting.

I think I was alone with my thoughts in that tiny room for twenty minutes or more. I did calm down a bit during that time, and when an officer came in to change the position of my handcuffed hands from behind my back to in front of my waist, I didn't resist. Soon after that, the door swung open and I was shocked to see Ali and Wissam. Ali walked straight in, but the officer refused entry to his brother. Wissam and I glared at each other; seeing him stopped at the door gave me some small satisfaction. Ali, however, kept coming towards me until he stood less than a metre away from me. It was the first time I'd seen him face to face since he'd taken Lahela and Noah from Australia. I wanted to shove him, shake him, kick him so hard. I badly wanted to hurt him. He, though, had *that* look. How could I forget it? And how would I ever forget the first words he said?

'What the fuck have you done?'

'What do you mean, what have *I* done? You were the one who made me do this. You broke your promise.'

Ali headed back to the door. It swung open and there were Lahela and Noah.

'Hello, babies,' he said in his daddy voice.

I was repulsed as I watched him pick up the children.

'I've missed you.'

The door shut, and all I could hear was mumbling outside.

The door opened again, and yet another officer came in.

'God be with you,' he said to me.

I interpreted that as, *You're in deep trouble now.* I shrugged my shoulders and asked him what he would do. I swore at Ali under my breath, then I stared numbly at the floor again. My eyes were killing me; it hurt to change focus or direction.

Another officer – or was it one of the many I had seen before? – came in and led me out of the room and into the one that held the *60 Minutes* crew. Stephen, Tara, Tangles and Ben were still handcuffed and sitting on the bed; from memory, I think Ben may have been on a chair at the end of the bed. One of the recovery men was also crammed in with them. They all looked exhausted and extremely sad. Ben, who appeared to be on the verge of tears, looked the most affected. Stephen was the most collected; I had come to know that he isn't an overly expressive person, but he is someone who cares deeply about others, and I could see that he felt the full weight of everyone's anguish. He is a good man.

I was sat down next to Tara and our inside hands were handcuffed together.

'I'm so sorry,' she whispered.

Stephen said the same.

'Where's Adam?' I asked.

'In a cell.'

I closed my eyes, because it was too upsetting to look at anyone.

The detective who arrested me at the apartment walked in and high-fived some of the officers, which was more than enough to set me off on another rant. What was he celebrating?

'How dare you? You've taken my children. How can you think you've done a good thing? I'm not a criminal. I didn't do anything wrong.'

I spat out the same desperate questions that the police had become used to hearing. The *60 Minutes* guys tried to comfort me.

'Ssh, Sally.'

An officer changed the position of my cuffed hands so they were tight behind my back.

'One year! One year without my children.'

I looked at the *60 Minutes* crew and saw that every one of them had tears in their eyes. What had I done? I was suddenly ashamed. I was only making things worse for everyone. I calmed down, and tried to collect my thoughts. It was time to wait. Yet again. *Yet again.*

The room turned into an ants' nest with police coming and going with bits of paper that grew into higher piles on a desk that was about two metres from the bed. In one of our quick whispered conversations, Tara and I agreed it was ridiculous. Paperwork, paperwork, paperwork. I know they were doing their jobs but every piece of paper felt like it was building a wall higher between me and my children. But that wasn't the worst of it. Periodically, Ali came in, stared at us and then walked out without speaking. Now that *was* ridiculous. How could he have open access in a police station to seemingly do whatever he liked? I didn't understand at all. He was all buddy-buddy with the police, with handshakes and high-fives, as if they'd done Ali a favour. It felt like a surreal circus, and amid it all I didn't know where Lahela and Noah were being kept. I wanted to scream.

At other times, I felt my head drop and jolt me awake again in a millisecond cycle of tiredness and false sleep. Tara asked me a number of times if I was okay. It's easy to have pre-conceived ideas about how famous people must live in their own bubble with other famous people: red carpets, celebrity parties, air kisses, huge salaries, no understanding of how the real world works. I know the reality of a working journalist is very different but the glamour of television makes it all seem so glossy. Now, however, handcuffed to Tara, I was beginning to realise that when we were both stripped back we were one and the same: each a person with a family, emotions and fears. I was grateful for Tara's understanding, and indeed the empathy and sympathy of the whole *60 Minutes* crew.

It must have been about 9.30pm, when the paperwork was still in full swing, that I was un-cuffed and taken into an interrogation room, with a few chairs and a table. Ali was there, already seated. Despite his earlier aggression and parades, I was hopeful that he wanted to have a sensible discussion about what we would do in the best interests of Lahela and Noah. Yes, I'd brought the issue to a head in dramatic fashion, but now it had to be time for a solution. We both had to remove our emotion and think only about the welfare of our children.

I sat down on the other side of the table to Ali. The officer stepped back, and stood guard. Ali looked at me and shook his head.

'What do you want to talk to me about?' I asked.

'I want to know what was going through your head.'

'Well, you took the kids, Ali. What choice did I have?'

'I didn't think you'd go through with it.'

When I asked him what he meant, he said he had seen emails, but didn't specify what these emails were. He also mentioned a name, but again didn't specify anything. He told me he'd been with detectives when he answered my call and that they'd traced the number back to Adam's name and googled him, so they knew what he was about. I pushed him about this, but he said no more. It both confused and worried me. Was Ali bluffing? There was no way he could have known what I'd planned. I'd followed Adam Whittington's instructions to the letter. But how could they trace a phone call so quickly? I tried to think clearly. My only thought was that he had somehow gained information from my iPad, which I'd given Lahela and Noah when they were taken to Lebanon. However, I was absolutely certain that the email account I used with recovery agencies wasn't on that iPad. There was no way he could know; no one would have betrayed me like that. Ali didn't talk more about any of it. He seemed to want to show he was in control. He said that if he had his way the *60 Minutes* crew were going to be jailed for a long time, and Adam would not see the light of day. I was horrified by his brutal coldness, and told him how pathetic the situation had become, and if he let me talk with Lahela and Noah we could sort everything out. But no, that approach wasn't on his agenda. He was out to intimidate me.

'I hope Brendan's a good dad; he's going to have to step up for a while, because you're going away for a long time too.'

He was so cold. It shouldn't have surprised me, because I knew that treatment well. There was no way through to him. Or so I thought. At some point he switched back to the recovery and asked if the children had been frightened and had asked for him.

'They were scared for a little while, but then Lahela realised I was there, and they were okay after that. Lahela kept telling Noah, "I told you Mummy would come and get us." I'm not trying to upset you, Ali, but they did not mention Daddy the entire time.'

For the first and only moment in our conversation, Ali's eyes welled up. Emotion. I flashed back to the gentleness he'd shown when Lahela and Noah were born. I used to cling to those thoughts when he was at his cruellest towards me, but now all gentleness was gone.

'Do you know what you've done to those children?' he asked.

I stared at him. What *I* had done? 'Can you understand that Lahela remembers me? She wants to know me, and Noah wants to know me. They want to know their mother.'

Ali was still upset, but he shrugged it off and moved on.

We said many things to each other. I'm writing here only about the words that have really haunted me since.

'How come you didn't try to take the kids when I was taking them to school?' he asked.

'Because I didn't want them to see us scuffling or arguing on the street. And that's what I thought would have happened.'

It was then that Ali gave an answer that I will never forget. He said that if he had been at the recovery he would have shot me.

'What, are you a gangster now? So, you would have shot me in front of the kids?'

'Yeah,' he replied. 'I'm done.'

I couldn't believe what he had said so matter-of-factly. He wanted to shoot me! And that was the end of it. Ali stood and spoke to the police officer, who obviously hadn't understood a word of our exchange. The officer then came over to put the handcuffs on me. It was ludicrous – was he taking orders from Ali? By this stage I was crying and trembling.

'Why, Ali? Why are you doing this?'

'It's okay, stop,' he said without feeling.

'It's not okay, Ali.'

Then he walked out, and I truly bawled. Would he even care if I disappeared forever? Would he care if I never saw Lahela and Noah again?

I was taken back to the room where the *60 Minutes* team and the local recovery guy had been handcuffed to the bed, but now only Tara remained. We were again handcuffed to each other.

'Where are the others?' I asked.

'In a cell.'

Tara looked as wrecked as I felt. She told me she and the crew had been at the station for twenty-four hours. Our sleeping spot for the night was the small single bed that the crew had been sitting on all that time; it was normally used by officers during breaks and between shifts. We tried to get as comfortable as we could by lying down head to toe in foetal positions with our cuffed hands on each other's knees. It was the only time we didn't have an officer in the room.

The room reeked of cigarette smoke. I had a massive headache, and despite being so tired, I found it hard to sleep. And whenever I did drift off, it was never long before I was woken by the pain of the handcuffs digging into my knee, or my arm being wrenched by Tara's regular flinching. I would wake up Tara to tell her, she would apologise and we would shift to some position of relative comfort, and then try to sleep again. Pins and needles; pains in the hip, knee and arms; and eyes that stung so badly it was as though they had been bitten.

At about 2am, there was a bang. We both jumped awake to see an officer smiling at us in the semi-darkness. He was obviously satisfied that there was some paperwork that needed to be put down with more force than others.

'Oh my God, did he have to be that loud?' whispered Tara after he'd gone.

By about 5am, all the lights were switched on and an officer asked us if we wanted a Nescafé. I told him I needed to use the toilet and brush my teeth, and I was un-cuffed and allowed to collect my brush and toothpaste from my bag in another room. Paranoid or not, I worried afterwards that I would get sick from using tap water.

Later in the morning, two representatives from the Australian embassy arrived. The senior official, Maggie, suggested I would be wise to obtain legal representation. Four months earlier I had contracted a Beirut lawyer, Ghassan Moghabghab, to deliver to Ali copies of the Australian court orders; Maggie agreed to contact him on my behalf. Channel Nine had arranged its own lawyer for the *60 Minutes* crew, and I presumed Adam was also seeking representation.

Maggie said she had spoken with my mum and Brendan and would talk with them again to let them know I was okay. She and her assistant, Pascal, were lovely and I was grateful to them both.

When my lawyer arrived, I was surprised, to say the least. I had never met Ghassan Moghabghab, and had only dealt with him via WhatsApp, where his profile picture showed him wearing a suit and holding a fat cigar. The photo was enough to convince me that he looked like a lawyer, but when I saw him in person he looked so friendly and nice. Not how I'd imagined him from his photo. Even when he wasn't smiling he looked as though he was. I needed that approachability and was glad I had chosen him. In contrast, Nine's representative walked in wearing a slick suit, sunglasses and an imposing air of superiority.

Ghassan gave me a little smile and told me he was preparing documents, and would soon be going back to his office to put together more paperwork. He gave me a description of what he was doing, and the only thing I really understood were his parting words: 'Good to finally meet you.'

That morning, there was one arrival that stood out above all others. Ali came, and as opposed to the previous night, he did not come close and eyeball me; instead, he stood across a crowded room, holding a blanket, pillow and food for me. He seemed to make sure everyone was watching and listening. This was the *concerned* Ali who was letting everyone know that he was looking after his poor, troubled wife. He kept asking me if I needed money to buy food. He must have said it half a dozen times, to the point that Tara urged me to accept his financial offering of about fifty Australian dollars. At that stage, I don't think she realised how Ali worked. And nor did the translator, who said to me: 'What is wrong with you? He seems a nice man.'

After creating the desired effect, Ali left, but only after loudly announcing that I was to call him if I needed anything else. I almost laughed. I needed our kids! What was he playing at? One day he was saying he would have shot me, then the next he was my personal charity. Games. Nothing but games. And the worrying thing was, I had a feeling worse was to come.

Chapter Twenty-two

On Friday, 8 April – two days after the recovery – Tara and I were moved to a detention centre near the police station. Adam, two other recovery agents and the rest of the *60 Minutes* crew were taken separately, at a different time, to the same place. There was a media scrum outside crowding to take pictures as Tara and I walked handcuffed together to a police car. By then, the story was front-page news in Australia, but in Beirut I couldn't grasp just how big the story had become. I was given some idea soon after we entered the centre, and saw a reporter from the ABC coming out. Tara recognised him, and they said hello to each other. The reporter asked if he could take a photo of her. She said no, and thanked him for having the courtesy to ask. The exchange was all very polite.

Although our previous night on the bed had been trying, it was absolute luxury compared with what we were about to experience. After passing through a locked prison gate we were escorted down a few flights of stairs to a room where all our belongings were thoroughly inspected by male guards. It had only been three months since I'd given birth to Eli, and I was still expressing milk; in a different circumstance the sight of a foreign man in uniform asking me to explain my breast pump would have been funny, but here, staring at uncertainty, I found it just another slope on a growing mountain of despair. I did, however, smile at Tara when she winced at the destruction of one of her expensive bras as a guard removed its underwire.

The guards made a list of all our valuables – jewellery, money, and so on – and put everything together in a safe. We were each allowed to keep our daily essentials, such as a blanket, toothbrush, toothpaste and some clothes. I had just one pair of pants and two T-shirts; later, Maggie came to the rescue with a few more bits and pieces.

The inspection – and one last chance to express milk – took about an hour. Then our handcuffs were removed and we were escorted along a dark, narrow passageway. We passed two cells that were full of male detainees; I couldn't see them because of the lack of light, but the sounds of their voices alone were very confronting. I would have rather died than be put in one of those boxes.

We reached a metal-grille door with a small window that had three bars across it. I looked at Tara, but neither of us spoke. The door was pushed back to reveal a cell that smelled of diesel. It was several metres long and a few metres wide. A generator throbbed away in the back corner near a squat toilet and a window slit that looked out onto dirt, presumably the ground outside. The only other light came from a single bulb on the ceiling. On closer inspection, I noticed either concrete or paint was peeling off some parts of the walls. So, this was going to be our home until further notice. A home with four other women who, I assumed, were in their twenties. Tara and I walked in and accustomed ourselves to the surrounds, or maybe it's better to say we just cringed. On one side was an area to store blankets and thin, grotty roll-up mattresses that I doubted had ever been washed; God only knows how many people had slept on them.

We met our cellmates and tried to hold a conversation with hand gestures, expressions, some English and Arabic. Once we worked out that the four were from Syria, it was time to try another obvious prison question.

'Why are you here?' I asked them.

They looked at each other and laughed.

'Night-time. Street,' one of them said in English.

I looked at Tara.

'I think they are . . .'

'Yes, I think they are too.'

We exchanged an awkward glance as the women laughed and joked in Arabic. A desperate mother, a journalist, and four Syrian prostitutes together. This was no place for division.

Tara and I took our mattresses out and arranged them on the floor. The Syrians had taken the best spots, furthest away from the toilet.

It was impossible to know how much time passed before a guard came in and took Tara and me upstairs to meet with Maggie. It was nice to hear another Australian accent, although many of the words spoken were grim. Maggie said there was little chance of us getting out in a hurry, and there was a very real possibility that we could be inside for a long time.

'Things are looking really dim, girls,' she said.

The only bright note was the copy of an email she brought from my mum. It said that all was good at home, and Eli was well.

We're hoping for the best and thinking of you always.

It was very matter of fact, and I knew Mum would have written it that way to avoid me worrying. But how could I not? My determination to bring Lahela and Noah back to Australia had affected so many people. Firstly, my family. I knew that Mum, Dad, Simon, Bryce and Lew would all get through in their own ways, but that didn't stop me from imagining their distress. I just wanted to tell them how sorry I was. I wanted to jump in a time machine and go back to when we all had Lahela and Noah happily in our lives. I wanted to go back and say no to Ali, without any guilt. If only. Then, what to say to Brendan? I took strength from knowing he was always so supportive, but now? How could I ever apologise? And Eli. God, I missed my baby, and this was where I really was messed up. I loved him but in a horribly weird way I felt I was almost cheating on Lahela and Noah by giving him that love. I felt I should be giving Lahela and Noah more of the share. When I left Australia, I was a little removed from Eli, as though I were saying to him, *Right, you stay where you are. I'm just going to get your brother and sister because they really need me.* Poor baby Eli. Just three months old. God, what had I done? And yet, the confusion in my head was also telling me that he was safe with Brendan and our families, so there was no need to worry. Whatever the reactions of all at home, the bottom line was that I had taken all my family to a point to which none of them should ever have been subjected.

And then there were the tormented thoughts about Adam and his men, and the *60 Minutes* crew. I had followed Adam's instructions to a T, so I still didn't know how we'd been caught. I had to remind myself that I didn't forcefully drag any of them into this mess, but there was still the very human part of me struggling with guilt. They had all been trying to help me, so I felt personally to blame. If I hadn't allowed Ali to take Lahela and Noah back to Beirut

I wouldn't have ever known what CARI was and *60 Minutes* would have remained a show to watch on Sunday night. But, in the context of the time, how could I not allow Ali to take his children to Beirut to see his family? I trusted him. And he promised me he would bring them back. Sitting in the cell, I knew my decision to let the kids go was the worst of my life, but at the time I felt that it was the right thing to do. So, again my mind whirred. Was I personally to blame for the mess? No, because it was Ali who lit the wick. He stopped me from seeing or speaking to my children; I merely responded to what he had done. Any blame I faced could only be attributed to a loving mother's desire to protect and nurture her children. All of this drama lay at Ali's feet.

After reading Mum's email and talking with Maggie and also Ghassan, it was back to the cell, where Tara's and my only contact with the outside world were the feet that occasionally passed by our window.

The generator – *the bloody generator* – became our most annoying companion. It was so loud. *Drrrrrrrrrrrrrrrrrr!* It would sound for half an hour, maybe more, then it would switch off and another generator would start further down the cell block. On, off, on, off . . . Every time the one in our cell was on I developed a headache that throbbed like the generator itself. Every time it was off it didn't take long to hear Stephen's low voice in the cell next to us. I imagined he and the others were in much worse conditions than we were.

Our only water supply came from a pipe on a wall. We needed to push a button, and out came the water, which we collected in a small plastic container. We then used the container to flush the toilet, and to wash. It was such a dirty, mucky area that I was grateful I had thongs to wear; Tara had only shoes, which she preferred to keep in the cleaner part of the cell, so I gave her my thongs whenever she needed to walk in the grime.

We managed to get a little uncomfortable sleep that night, and in the morning, Saturday, we were greeted by a friendly female guard who came in to check on us, and presumably make sure we hadn't done the impossible and escaped. Then again, maybe it was possible because on one day – I think Saturday but I can't be sure – Tara and I were surprised when we heard, 'Hello, hello,' coming from outside our cell.

'Who's that?' Tara asked me. 'The guards don't speak English, do they?'

She looked through the door window to see a man standing there. He introduced himself as Pierre.

'Your Australian friends. They are really nice,' he said.

He told her that he was in the same cell as the crew. Apparently Stephen, Ben and Tangles had been taken upstairs to receive an update from Maggie, but the guards had forgotten to lock their cell door, so Pierre decided to visit us. He was a chirpy, quirky character – I think half-American, half-French – who didn't seem the least concerned about being caught outside his cell. I was wary of becoming involved, so I lay on my mattress while Pierre chatted. Tara suggested he should return to his cell, which he eventually did, again seemingly without any worry about possible consequences. It was another bizarre moment to add to a growing list.

Saturday was also the first time I saw Adam since he had left the safe house. We passed each other in the passageway leading to upstairs, where Tara and I were being taken to meet Maggie. There was no time for anything more than, 'Are you okay?' and a quick answer. Then Adam went back to his cell, and Tara and I went on to hear Maggie tell us that there was talk of us facing up to twenty years' imprisonment. I refused to believe this. How could I? Acceptance would have seen me spiral down further. Things would work out somehow. They had to. I had to believe that.

When back in our cell, we cleaned the floor with mops and an anti-bacterial wash that the guards gave us. This was to be a daily occurrence. Later, the Syrian women were all taken away; if I understood them properly, they were going to prison in Tripoli. The cell was much quieter without them and, thankfully, there was a lot more space for Tara and me. As we set about moving our camp as far away from the toilet as possible, a huge hairy spider, about half the size of my hand, walked out from under my mattress. I had never seen one as large in my life, and I freaked out. It wasn't scared of us at all, making its way slowly across the floor as though it owned the place while I jumped up and down in panic.

'Kill it, Tara, kill it!'

That set Tara off too, and no doubt our shrieks were heard along the cell block.

'Get a shoe, Sally!'

I picked up one of my thongs, but we decided it was too flimsy for the job. I found one of Tara's shoes, a ballet-type slipper.

'Kill it, Sally.'

'I'm not doing it. I'm not going near it.'

I gave Tara the slipper and she whacked the spider once but it didn't even flinch. She hit it again. And again. It still kept on walking.

'Hit it hard!'

'I am!'

Tara must have had about ten goes at it before it looked half-squished, although it was still moving. Tara finally put her shoe on and with a good stomp our visitor was finally dead. I got our one and only roll of toilet paper, and gave Tara a square. She picked up the spider and dropped it into the toilet.

'Oh my God, I was sleeping on that thing, Tara. Is this going to be our life?'

'I hope not. This is horrible.'

We both started to laugh *and* cry. Relief and the sheer desperation of our situation couldn't be separated. Before settling, we shook our mattresses and everything else we had to check for more spiders. That incident brought me closer to Tara. I looked back at our initial meeting and interview in Brisbane when she said she wanted to get to know me better. Well, that was happening, wasn't it? All the glamour had been stripped away, replaced by the rawness of reality in a Beirut prison cell. Throughout it all, though, were unexpected reminders of our lives on the outside, and none were more eye-raising to me than Tara's clothes: how they remained un-crinkled will always remain one of the mysteries of prison life. No matter what, she was still always graceful.

We spent the rest of the day reading books that Maggie had given us, and when bored of that, we did a gym workout of squats, stretches and yoga, complete with made-up names like *The Flamingo* for our poses. At times I wondered if I was having something close to an out-of-body experience, and I was looking down on myself in utter disbelief as I stood on one leg talking and joking in a prison cell. It was just so ridiculous. Then something would snap me back into the real world. Most often it was the generator. But it too had its farcical side. The only electricity needed in our cell was for the single light bulb that was on 24/7. Of course I knew the generator would power other parts of the building, but when the *Drrrrrrrrrrrrrrrrr* started it was hard not to look at the light bulb and think, *That's a lot of noise for forty watts.*

That night was bitterly cold. I crawled under my one blanket wearing the few clothes I had, and hoped that the thin mattress would be enough to keep the chill of the concrete away. Tara lay on her mattress alongside me, with our newly made library stack close by. I remember waking up at one point because my feet were cold. Then again, it might have been because of the generator starting, or the light bulb shining in my eyes, or a bad dream.

The next morning the friendly guard came again for her inspection and to give a gift: hot water for the Nescafé sachets that Maggie had given Tara and me. The guard said in broken English that she could only do it once; if she was caught it would be 'very, very bad'. Tara and I were extremely grateful. The coffee wasn't good, but it warmed us up and made a change from the Arabic bread we had been living on. Eating any of the other food that was delivered by a guard each morning was a gamble. So far we had been given boiled potatoes with the skin and dirt still on them, and some boiled eggs, the first of which I hungrily cracked in a hurry only to be put off by a disgustingly rotten smell that was made worse by a rising stench in the toilet. It seemed that Tara and I were going to lose weight until we were released.

Sunday was a 'no visit' day, so we resigned ourselves to long hours of reading, chatting, trying to sleep, and doing the occasional stretch. Our situation was relatively bearable until six new women joined us. All were young – in their twenties – and had been given cigarettes by the guards, and Tara and I spent the rest of the day in a headache-inducing cloud of smoke.

As we had done with the prostitutes, we tried to start a conversation, and from what we could gather, the women had illegally come across the Syrian border. From the moment they arrived in the cell, they didn't stop talking. And smoking. There wasn't even a break when I let them know that Tara and I were settling down for the night.

'We should make as much noise as them,' I complained.

'Yes, I think we should.'

After I finally managed to drift off, it didn't take long before I was awake again thanks to a poorly placed foot that landed on me when someone was walking to the toilet.

'Ssh!' I complained.

The women giggled.

It was a long night.

Would I ever get used to this?

I hoped not.

Chapter Twenty-three

The smell of stale cigarette smoke was in my hair and clothes, the mattresses, the air, everywhere. What a nauseating way to begin another day. Monday, 11 April. When in a prison cell it doesn't take long to realise that you aren't only trapped by the walls around you, but the routine you make for yourself, and which is made for you by authorities. After only three nights in the detention centre I was becoming increasingly agitated. I was worried about Eli and Brendan, and I couldn't stop thinking about Lahela and Noah. What were they thinking? And what had Ali told them about me? Surely something had to happen soon?

Some sort of answer came when the friendly guard escorted Tara and me upstairs for our regular get-together with Maggie and Pascal. When we walked into our meeting room we saw two new people who were very familiar to Tara, but complete strangers to me: Channel Nine's news director, Darren Wick, and Sallie Stone, a security consultant contracted by the network. They were very keen to talk with Tara, but their problem was that I was handcuffed to their star reporter. So, they had to make do as best they could. It was a very weird situation and they barely acknowledged me. Instead, they asked Tara how she was, and what she needed. They also said they were 'working' on things. It was only later that I learned that at this stage it was being reported that Channel Nine was trying to distance itself from the whole affair and was denying it had paid any money to CARI. And although I didn't know it then, this approach had fired up Brendan even more so back in Brisbane. After he first heard news reports of Nine's denials, he wrote a firm email to *60 Minutes*' Executive Producer, Kirsty Thomson, and Producer, Steve Burling. Brendan was obviously furious when he wrote and sent it off quickly, spelling mistakes and all:

8 April

Dear Steve & Kirsty,

As you are aware there are continued reports being made in the media by your network that Sally had paid and organised CARI to carry out the recovery and [sic] Lahela and Noah. As you are also aware this is completely untrue I have evidence to the contrary which confirms the whole operation was paid for and organised by Channel 9 and 60 minutes. We both know Sally was not operating independently and any suggestion by you other [sic] *is outrageous.*

Sally has now been arrested by Lebanese authorities and the untrue and false reports being made by you are placing her is [sic] *very serious position which could have very serious consequences. I understand your position by trying to distance yourself from the situation to assist your staff however you cannot do it at the expense of Sally and her liberty.*

I am quite prepared to provide that evidence I have to the Australian Government, the Lebanese authorities and to other media outlets unless all reports suggesting Sally organised and paid for the operation and [sic] *removed immediately. I also advise that evidence will be released if any further untrue statements are made moving forward. Be advised It* [sic] *will also be released to the Australian and Lebanese authorities in the event it will assist with Sally's release and possible defense* [sic].

I ask that you confirm all reports have been removed by 11am today or I will be speaking with other media outlets.

Kind regards,
Brendan Pierce

Brendan received a reply and a phone call from Kirsty that managed to calm him down. He didn't go through with his threat; he was just extremely worried about the consequences for me. He felt so helpless so far away and I couldn't contact him so he obsessed on the media reports – many of which were wrong. Thousands of miles away, I, not knowing what was happening back at home, was left wondering if Darren and Sallie would ever give me more than the time of day.

My main priority was to speak with my lawyer, Ghassan, who said he was working flat-out gathering material for my defence.

'Sally, this is very big news in Lebanon. It's not good for your case.'

He tried to soften the blow by telling me he had been in contact with Brendan several times on WhatsApp, and all was well with my family in Brisbane. Judging by Brendan's email it obviously wasn't, but I didn't know that.

No sooner had I spoken with Ghassan than in walked Ali, and again he turned on the theatrics by asking in front of everyone if I needed anything. I knew that people were staring at me, and I got the vibe that at least some of them shared the translator's opinion. I felt like I could read their thoughts: *What is wrong with this woman? Her husband seems so nice.* I desperately wanted to tell him where to go, but that would have only made me seem crazy – or crazier – in the minds of those who had doubts about me. So, I was very polite.

'No, I'm fine thank you, Ali.'

'Okay.'

Then he left, and I was again left feeling upset and vulnerable.

'Don't cry. If you cry, I cry,' said the friendly guard.

What beautiful words from someone on 'the other side'. That guard was so lovely. I only wish I knew her name. Her kindness helped.

During our next chat with Maggie, she asked us how we were coping 'under the circumstances'.

'It's interesting down there,' replied Tara.

'Yes, I could imagine.'

Maggie asked us if we needed more books, but I told her I would prefer some light magazines.

'I'll see what I can do.'

Despite the seriousness in the room, there was a touch of Monty Python too. The commander who oversaw everything just happened to be extremely handsome, and prompted any number of women to comment: 'He is *very* good-looking isn't he?' There were no arguments from any of us.

Such moments were welcome distractions for me. Each new meeting and discussion stretched me in some way or other, and even the lighter conversations were draining. And the most demanding of the day was still to come.

We were still upstairs waiting to go back to the cell when I was un-cuffed from Tara and led by the friendly guard through an open door into a large office. I didn't know what to expect. One of the first things I noticed was a TV in a corner that showed CCTV footage of the hallway outside. In another corner, a man with intense eyes sat behind a desk; he was busily writing away on a notepad, and I assumed he was a transcriber.

I had taken just a few steps when two police officers moved into position at the entrance. My lawyer, Ghassan, walked alongside me and we stopped only metres from Ali and his lawyer. I couldn't look at my estranged husband. His presence immediately unsettled me, and I felt my eyes begin to burn with tears. We all stood in front of a desk that was dominated by a mountain of paperwork, presumably the same mountain that had started as a single sheet in the police station. Behind the desk sat a man, probably in his thirties, smartly dressed. In all the meetings I would have with him from this day, he wore a suit but sometimes took his jacket off, rolled up his sleeves and undid the top button of his crinkle-free white shirt. He had an obvious air of authority. He was Judge Rami Abdullah.

I was struggling to hold it together. Judge Abdullah noticed my discomfort and spoke gently to me. I immediately liked him. I only hoped beyond hope that he would see reason in my actions, because he was the man responsible for investigating the recovery and determining the fate of so many: me, the *60 Minutes* crew, Adam and his men, and the precious ones at the centre of it all, Lahela and Noah.

I listened to Judge Abdullah tell me, in very good English, the charges I was facing: article 495, kidnapping; article 554, harming and making injuries; and some other offence related to assisting in an alleged crime. His words frightened me. Before I walked into that room enough people had told me of the gravity of the situation – I knew it myself too – but right from my childhood, as early as peas spilled on a floor, it had been in my nature to assume that everything would work out well in the end. Despite all that had happened since I had arrived in Beirut I still clutched to that belief. Yes, I was probably still in the ultimate state of denial, but how else to look at the situation? Sitting listening to each and every word of Judge Abdullah, I just *could not* believe I was now facing the prospect of going to prison for twenty years. That happened to other people, but not me. Surely?

Judge Abdullah told me he understood my situation, but stressed that what I had done was very wrong, and there were many more appropriate ways for me to have tried to gain access to Lahela and Noah.

'Really?' I asked. I wasn't being disrespectful, I just didn't know what more I could have done when Ali wouldn't communicate.

He told me I could have gone through the courts. Given that Lebanon wasn't a member of the Hague Convention I wasn't sure where I stood but hearing what he said gave me hope.

Judge Abdullah asked me a lot of questions, many of which I had already been pressed on by the police immediately after my arrest: 'Why did you do this?' 'Who was in the car with you?' 'What was the arrangement with Adam?' And so on. I was truthful and candid. Occasionally I lost my train of thought, but after about an hour, Judge Abdullah thanked me, and then I was on my way back with Tara to our cell.

The next day we passed the hours reading, chatting, whinging to each other about our loud cellmates, and of course we passive smoked. We were both tired and grumpy. There were more meetings for us upstairs, and in news that broke the cycle of routine we were told Judge Abdullah would hold a hearing the following day.

That night, the thunder echoed in the mountains, and I woke up to see feet walking through puddles in the world outside. As I mentioned in Chapter One, this was a gut-wrenching moment: it is excruciating to know that you are at your happiest in life when you are asleep. Waking up to the knowledge that you are trapped in a day, a week, a month, or a whole lifetime where pain and torment are always with you is surely one of the worst experiences a human being can endure. But was I at my lowest point yet? I don't know. I'll never know.

Later, when I again fronted Judge Abdullah I was on the edge of a breakdown. More questions, more answers, and more trembling at the sight of Ali. Judge Abdullah urged us to resolve matters between us; obviously I was desperate to, but Ali had other ideas. Among the judge's considerable prompting and suggestions one took me completely off-guard: he asked me to apologise to Ali.

'Sorry?' I asked.

'No, not to me, but to Ali,' said Judge Abdullah.

'I don't want to apologise.'

'I understand your point of view, but I don't think you have an option, considering the circumstances you are in.'

Reluctantly, I turned to Ali, who was less than two metres away from me.

'Sorry.'

'Sorry for what?' pushed Judge Abdullah.

'Ali, sorry for trying to get my children back.'

There was no meaningful response from Ali, and Judge Abdullah could see it was pointless pushing any further. I already knew enough about the Lebanese legal process to realise that Ali held a lot of power. If he'd suddenly put his hands up and said, 'Enough is enough, let's move on,' he would have made Judge Abdullah's job easier. But no. He was in for a fight, and he said to me just before he left the room: 'I'll see you in jail.'

I was escorted outside the office to find what I'd already seen on the judge's CCTV monitor: a hallway filled with media. Ali was already there. I glared at him and thought:

Look at me, you bastard. Look at me. But he was too busy texting someone; I felt he was doing anything to avoid making eye contact with me. I couldn't stop thinking about how cold he was. Before I knew it, I started to cry, and I immediately heard the *ch-ch-ch* of a camera clicking.

'Who took that?' I asked angrily. I didn't want Brendan or my mum to see that photo of me looking so emotional.

No one confessed.

'Whoever took that, please delete it.'

I looked around and saw a young woman who had guilt written all over her face.

'Did you take it?' I asked her.

An Australian male reporter, who appeared to be working with the woman, came across to me and said: 'Don't you know who I am?'

'No, and I don't care. I just want that photo deleted, please.'

He looked at me for a few moments and then he spoke with the woman without giving any indication of heeding my request.

'Excuse me, can you delete that photo, please?'

I burst into tears, and finally Ali saw me.

'What's wrong?' he asked.

I thought: *Why do you care all of a sudden?* Ali's unpredictable behaviour was only making me worse. He was hot, cold, switching his emotions on and off. I was such a wreck, there were moments when I actually felt sorry for him. With my voice trembling, I explained to Ali what had happened. Ali in turn spoke in Arabic to a police officer, who then walked over to the woman and grabbed her phone and flicked through the pictures. I don't know whether he deleted any, but she was far from impressed when he gave the phone back. And the male reporter shot me a filthy look before he left. I now accept that the woman was doing her job, but at the time . . . well, I was very fragile.

And that fragility was about to come under even greater pressure in a new environment where a healthy amount of personal space was no more than the width of a bunk bed.

Chapter Twenty-four

The holding cell at the detention centre was a long, thin room with a window at one end and bars that were spaced at least six inches apart. I joked with Tara that we were skinny enough to escape, but then we stuck our heads through the gaps and looked down at what we'd have to jump onto about three metres below us. There was a mass of rubbish that advertised hepatitis. I then looked elsewhere and saw little more than a fence with swirling barbed wire.

'We're stuck again.'

Every now and again guards would peer in at us; some would smile, others would just stare.

'I feel like we're animals in a zoo,' I said to Tara.

'I've felt like that from the beginning.'

We weren't there long before the door swung back and in came the guards.

'*Yalla, yalla* [Hurry, hurry].'

In another touch of Monty Python we were put in a ridiculously big, old truck with rickety wooden seats in a caged space at the back that would have fitted 100 people, maybe more. I looked into the driver's cabin and through the windscreen, and saw a swarm of media outside. Judge Abdullah had told us he wanted to minimise our exposure to the cameras, so perhaps this truck was his idea. It definitely stopped us from being photographed. The journey lasted only a minute up a hill.

We arrived at the Baabda Women's Prison, our new home. Judge Abdullah had told us of our change of residence only hours before, at the hearing. As at the detention centre, we endured another extensive search of our belongings, and I was lucky to be spared the indignity of an intrusive personal examination. It made me feel sick, just thinking about it. The supervising guard in charge stalked around in very high heels and wore a deathly stare that warned us not to get on the wrong side of her.

Despite her unnerving presence, there was some lightness in the circumstances. Before Tara and I arrived, Maggie had given us letters, printed emails and pictures from our families at home. These meant a great deal to Tara and me; I wasn't the only one missing my kids, Tara was missing hers badly too. Having something from my home life that I could touch and hold onto was as precious a gift as I could have received at that time. I looked at photos Brendan had taken of Eli, and I tried to remember the last time I held him. Was it really only twelve days ago that I'd said goodbye to him? Would he ever get to meet his brother and sister?

Those little gifts became even more important to me after a guard announced that Tara and I were being put in different cells. I immediately felt panic rise in me; Tara had become such a pillar of strength, I was petrified how I would get on without her. I wanted to try and support her too. But Tara was so strong throughout the whole ordeal.

'You'll be okay,' Tara assured me. 'We'll get through this.'

It was early evening by the time I arrived at Cell 3. All but one of the fourteen inmates was sitting on the floor having a communal dinner; the other was sitting by herself eating bread rolls. Everyone looked at me as I walked in. Lebanese, Syrian, African . . . some older than fifty, many in their twenties. I didn't know where to go or what to do. I sat down by myself, too afraid to speak. The cell was vastly different from the one at the detention centre. It was about thirty square metres and had the look of a school dormitory. There were a few bunk beds pushed up against walls already crowded with a reverse-cycle air-conditioner and cupboards for personal belongings, food and cooking utensils. There was a mat in the middle of the floor, a television in a corner, and towards the back was a curtain that partially hid a toilet and shower area.

I don't know how long I sat there waiting for something to happen. But the more time passed, the more I felt Tara was wrong. No, I wouldn't be okay. I wouldn't get through this. No one was talking to me and I didn't know what to do. Again, I began to cry. An older woman, probably fifty-five, stared at me. She wore jeans and a T-shirt; her hair was grey, she had heavy wrinkles under her eyes, and some of her fingers were stained with nicotine.

'Stop, stop,' she said in Arabic. Then she asked one of the African women, who spoke some English, to ask me what I had done to be here.

'I'm from Australia. My estranged husband took my children, and I came here to get them back.'

After hearing the translation, a number of the inmates nodded, and chatted away. My basic understanding of what they were saying was: 'She's the girl on the news.' In the to and fro of translations that followed, nearly everyone in the cell apparently agreed with my behaviour, and some said they would have done exactly the same thing.

I was soon shown my sleeping place, which as expected was determined by hierarchy. Those who had been there the longest had the bunks, and the shortest stayers were given spaces on mattresses on the floor between the bunks. I put down my blanket and pillow, which had both been given to me by Ali during one of his acts of 'kindness'. Quite simply, I had needed a blanket and so I had accepted it.

I settled on my bed to watch and listen. It was obvious that the older woman who had broken the silence with me – I would come to know her as Mumma – was the boss of the cell. Mumma was the only person allowed to touch the television's remote control and change channels, and when she spoke, no one talked over her. I wondered what she had done to be in this place. In fact, it was human nature for me to be curious about what *everyone* had done. Was I in with murderers, robbers, drug dealers? How could I tell one from another? And how would they treat me for however long I was with them? I started thinking about Tara. I hoped she was okay. And the rest of the crew.

I had a broken night's sleep – I kept waking with thoughts of Lahela and Noah but eventually exhaustion stopped my mind whirring. I woke the next morning to a great surprise: breakfast in bed – cucumber, tomato, Arabic bread and curdled yoghurt – delivered by another older woman who wasn't even from our cell. She had braided hair and wore a T-shirt that had a picture of Bob Marley on it. Along with the feast she handed me a note written in English. I couldn't believe it when I read that the food was from another Australian inmate who had been told there were two new Aussies in the prison. She didn't know who we were, but she was looking forward to meeting us 'upstairs'.

I didn't know what she meant, but later in the day I found out when my cellmates and I were escorted up to the prison rooftop to a fenced-off recreation yard that was about half the size of a tennis court. It was here that four cells of inmates, about sixty women, were taken at any one time for two hours a day. Once there, most prisoners sat around in little groups and talked.

Much to my relief, Tara was up there with me, and we found a spot and began to swap stories about our cells and cellmates. It didn't take long for our breakfast benefactor to come over and introduce herself. To say she was astounded to see Tara was an understatement. There is no need for me to mention her name, nor tell you how she found herself behind bars so far from home, but I must say that she was very kind to us both. She said she was expecting to be released in a couple of months, and was in countdown mode after a lengthy imprisonment. Knowing she was looking out for us was a heartening thing.

Apart from having sunlight, space and Tara's company, one of the greatest joys of being on the rooftop was having room to hang my clothes out to dry. I had handwashed them in the cell, and I don't think many readers could imagine the immense satisfaction I got from wringing out the stench of generator diesel and cigarette smoke from my stay in the detention centre.

That day, Thursday, 14 April, was a very busy one. After time on the rooftop, I was taken to an interview room and was asked standard paperwork questions by a woman from Lebanon's Ministry of Justice: 'What is your birthday?' 'How many children do you have?' The only question that brought a double-sided answer was: 'Are you married?' Yes, technically I was, but I wanted it to be known that I had separated from my husband. I don't know how that was recorded on the files.

I also had an unexpected interaction after the guards told me that my sister was waiting in the visitors' room to see me. Of course I didn't have a sister, and so I wasn't interested in solving the mystery of who the person could be. It was either a mistake or a set-up. However, the guards demanded I meet the person, so I was taken to a room where I stood at a bench table behind a panel of glass. On the other side stood a woman I didn't recognise. She had messy blonde hair that she continually brushed out of her face as she spoke to me, introducing herself as a reporter from News Limited. I told her I wouldn't comment about the story, but after prompting, I gave her a message for my family. Although she didn't pass that message on personally, I did find out later that she put some relevant quotes into an article that was billed as an exclusive:

'Please tell my mum and dad how well I am and also Brendan and my in-laws . . .'

'I am fine but my loved ones need to know that.'

The Australian newspaper, 15 April 2016

Much of the rest of my first full day in prison was spent getting the feel for cell routine. At about 4pm everyone sat down for a communal meal of tabouli, potato chips, salad and bread. It had been prepared by Mumma, who was given special privileges to do all the cooking for us in a little kitchen on the rooftop. This was her daily job, and I assumed it was her choice to do it. Everyone in the cell was expected to contribute food items, which could be ordered from an official shopping list that was distributed every two weeks. I was told that since an order had only just been received, I didn't have to supply anything. Mumma and many of the others were adamant that was the way it should be, and there was no doubt that Mumma had taken a liking to me. In her very broken English, she had already been candid with me about having some sort of Mafia links, and had been in the prison for fifteen years with no chance of getting out any time soon. She was, without question, a bit of a hard arse, but she was lovely to me and I will always appreciate that.

While we ate dinner we watched a news bulletin on TV, and it wasn't long before my face popped up on the screen. Someone translated for me: there would be more court procedures on Monday, four days away. It was an interesting way for me to find out, and made me wonder just how much I didn't know about what was going on.

That night, I was still edgy about being the new girl. The woman who slept next to me made me even more anxious. She was another older Lebanese woman who slept on the bunk below Mumma's, which meant she was only inches away from my floor space. Considering the glares she gave me during the day, I was worried what she might do to me in the darkness. Luckily, she only intruded on my space by blowing cigarette smoke in my direction. She smoked a lot at night. Many of the women did.

Very early in the morning, I was startled awake by the cries of a baby. At first I thought I was dreaming, but the sound continued. A baby in the prison? Everyone else was asleep, but how could I rest while such a familiar sound echoed along the corridor? I immediately thought about Eli. Stuck in a Beirut prison, did I suddenly have more of a chance of seeing Lahela and Noah again than I did of seeing Eli? The terror of that thought felt almost like a physical blow. Would I ever see my baby again? I tormented myself by imagining Eli and Brendan at home without me, and the possibility that I wouldn't get out. I had failed to get Lahela and Noah back and now I'd lost Eli and Brendan too. What if I never got out? That could actually happen, couldn't it? And if it did, what scars would all three of my children bear? I would have damaged them all by not being there for them.

My anguish carried on long after the baby's cries stopped. My thoughts were a jumble of living nightmares as I kept questioning myself, what I'd done, what I could have done better. And then I would hear Lahela's voice: 'Mummy, I want to come home.' What choice did I have? None. I did what I did because I had promised to bring my children home. I hoped Eli would forgive me and understand when he was older. I worried about Brendan, too. He was so supportive and loving, but what if it all got too much for him? Could he walk away with our son, and leave me completely alone? I lay on that thin mattress and started to quietly cry. I could have said no when Ali asked to take Lahela and Noah on holiday. I could have said no when Channel Nine said it would pay for the recovery. I could have, should have, would have, couldn't have, shouldn't have, wouldn't have . . . If I stayed for too long in this prison, I knew I would eventually go mad.

When morning came, there was no extravagant breakfast, but I had other surprises to help carry me through the day. Stephanie, a volunteer church worker who regularly visited the prison, gave me a pile of letters and cards from members of the Beirut Baby Mamas. I read them on the rooftop:

269

'*Like many others here and in Australia I have been devastated to learn that you, as a loving mother, have been prevented from raising your children. What I hear of what has happened is a terrible injustice and my heart is breaking for you. Please know that I am praying for you, Noah and Lahela.*

I shared your story with my bible study group last night. The whole group joined together and was moved to pray for you. One of my friends prayed not only for you and Noah and Lahela, but that your case would lead in time to a change of laws that would protect other mothers and their children in the future.'

'*. . . for a mother to be denied her own children is so profoundly wrong, it stands against nature itself. It defies logic, morality, and humanity's most basic principles.*

Over the past week I've been thinking about you every day, finding it hard to sleep at night, only imagining what you and your children must be going through at this time.'

'*I cannot tell you how much I admire your strength. You have been put through an absolute hell already and now the best thing so far is that your kids already know how much you love them, that you are most definitely waiting for them, and that you have not abandoned them. You are STRONG and you will definitely come out of this even stronger.*'

'There are many cases like yours, where kids are taken away unfairly, from their moms. But you were strong enough to let the world know about your story. This is how much you love your kids, and this is why now, we all want to do something, anything to help you get out of this situation and go back to your kids.'

The boost I felt from the letters didn't last long, because when I returned to the cell nearly everyone was in a foul mood. There were arguments, and pushes and shoves that nearly came to fisticuffs. Apparently I was the cause of one disagreement when the woman who didn't like me told someone else that I was being treated too well for a new girl. It all fizzled out with no real harm done, but I kept a low profile, and spent most of my time numbly watching TV, or reading photocopies of newspaper articles about the whole recovery drama that Maggie had brought in for Tara and me. I also started to use the back of them to keep a rough diary of events.

On Saturday, 16 April, my lawyer, Ghassan, visited me and confirmed that we would be in court again on Monday. Brendan had sent him more than 200 emails I had written to Ali ever since Lahela and Noah had left Brisbane. Most revealed how hard I had tried to contact Ali and gain some sort of access to the children. Ghassan planned to present the emails to Judge Abdullah. He also confirmed that Brendan had deactivated the 'Bring Lahela and Noah home' Facebook page, due to some horrible comments posted on the page. Although there were thousands of messages of support for me, the vindictive and very personal assaults overrode all the positives. I didn't realise at the time, but Brendan had to delete every single member individually before he could close the page down.

Back in the cell, I had fallen into somewhat of a routine with a Brazilian woman named Ketney who had been supportive and friendly. She had been in prison for more than a year waiting to see if she would be charged with drug offences. We were partly drawn to each other because we were both mothers who were missing their kids; Ketney had two boys at home in Brazil. Because my bed was on the floor, it was rolled up and packed away during the day to allow more space, so Ketney invited me up to sit on her top bunk, and we had become so comfortable with each other that we spent hours chatting. She spoke reasonably good English, and was keen to add an Australian flavour to her vocabulary, so I taught her some really stupid old-fashioned expressions. After she mastered a few particular ones, we both got a laugh whenever she announced she was going to the toilet: 'Stone the flamin' crows, I'm bustin'.' Ketney was very religious and prayed every morning. She was my closest cellmate.

I got on with most of the prisoners pretty well. On Sunday, 17 April, some African women braided my hair, and shaped

Tara's as well on the only day of the week we were allowed to use blow-dryers. It served as a useful purpose for the Africans, who were undertaking a beautician's course run in the prison, while for Tara and me it was a nice distraction.

By then Tara and I had any number of stories to swap about the crimes that those in the prison had allegedly committed. Many of the African women were maids who had been accused of stealing from their employers. Their offences were often the minor ones in a place that was full of barbaric stories. There was one woman who, according to all the whispers, had been inside for much of her life after hacking her mother-in-law's head off and carrying it around her neighbourhood. Another had apparently chopped up a boy and cooked him before stabbing the boy's mother to death. I felt sick hearing such stories, but I wasn't afraid. Maybe having my own situation to worry about stopped me from spiralling into paranoia.

I did, however, recognise the prisoners to avoid. They were the ones with the empty look in their eyes. We had one in our cell. She was about seventy and kept to herself. She didn't take part in the communal meals or rostered cleaning that involved everyone except her and Mumma. Most of the time she said nothing, looked at no one, and during my term in Cell 3 she did not once go up to the rooftop. She just sat in the cell and barely moved. Tara had a different tragedy in her cell: a Syrian woman who didn't have the correct papers. She was pregnant with her tenth baby, and had the sorriest expression on her face. Whenever Tara and I were on the rooftop, this woman came and sat next to us and cried. If we moved, she would too; she was always there, nearly always crying. I told Tara I couldn't cope with the poor woman; Tara had no choice because she slept next to her at night, where the misery continued.

Of all the horrible stories and miserable characters, none affected me more than the mother whose baby I had heard crying in the night. She had apparently bashed her intellectually delayed step-daughter to death in a shower. Her husband – and father of the victim – wanted nothing to do with either his wife or their baby. It goes without saying that the woman needed to be punished, but the baby? She had already been born into a heart-breaking life.

As for my three children? I couldn't look any further than Monday, 18 April.

Chapter Twenty-five

Handcuffs, media, Judge Abdullah in his crinkle-free shirt, and Ali with no intention of speaking to me or looking at me. Monday, 18 April 2016 looked like being the same as my previous experiences in the judge's office. However, there was one big difference: Judge Abdullah said that everyone was trying hard to come to an 'agreement'. I didn't know what he meant, but I did feel encouraged. So did Tara, who said to me before we left: 'Well, that sounds promising.'

Earlier, I had given my lawyer, Ghassan, a letter I had received from Stephanie, the volunteer church worker at the prison. Written by another lawyer, it suggested Ghassan was taking the wrong approach to my case and should have been putting more effort into the rights of custody. After reading it, Ghassan shook his head.

'I know more about the story than anybody. It's easy for people to judge on the outside. This isn't about custody. This is a criminal case, and we need to get through this first.'

I didn't question Ghassan; I trusted him to do what he had to. And I hoped his efforts would lead to positives in both criminal *and* custody matters. In the meantime, it was back to prison for Tara and me.

What followed was the most bizarre day I've ever had in my life. This time, our one-minute trip up the hill to the prison was to be by car. Our trip down earlier should have been a warning: we had been taken from the vehicle one at a time, and were pushed and shoved by police officers until we were inside the detention centre and safe from the media that had begun to stampede down the hill from the prison after catching sight of us. Judge Abdullah said he didn't want a repeat of that, so he instructed plain-clothes detectives to take us through the back door of the detention centre when we left. We had to go down a flight of stairs, passing some media who were prevented from getting too close to us by officers but nevertheless they still fired questions at us: 'How do you feel, Sally?' 'What are conditions like in prison, Tara?'

Then Ali made his way past, and gave me a long glare before he walked away from us.

'That didn't look very friendly,' said Tara.

Lahela, Ali, me and baby Noah.
My family. I thought we were going
to be okay.

My grandmother with Noah (*below left*).

My mum with Noah (*below right*).

Beirut, August 2013 (*top left*): I was terrified the day a car bomb went off close to home and Ali and Lahela were nearby. I couldn't contact Ali and imagined the worst. That day made me realise I needed my children to grow up in a place where bombings and war weren't so close. I wanted them safe. Bringing them home to Australia meant they would be, and my mum was there to support us.

The end of my marriage was hard, but being great parents was all that mattered.
I thought Ali and I were doing well and putting the kids first. I loved every second I
spent with Lahela and Noah and being their mum is a joy.

My little tiger girl (*top*). Lahela, Noah and I spent our days adventuring together. Noah used to wear a pair of Lahela's tights whenever we went to the Chipmunks play centre to protect him on the slide (*below right*). I took this photo after a mammoth session – we got home and he crawled onto the bed and fell asleep with the cat before I could even get the tights off.

Ali travelled back and forth from Beirut and he always had contact with our children. We'd all spend time together when he was here, at places like Currumbin Wildlife Sanctuary (*above*). I thought everything was okay. I had no idea what was going on in his mind – and I found out too late.

Uncle Simon and Lahela (*below left*).

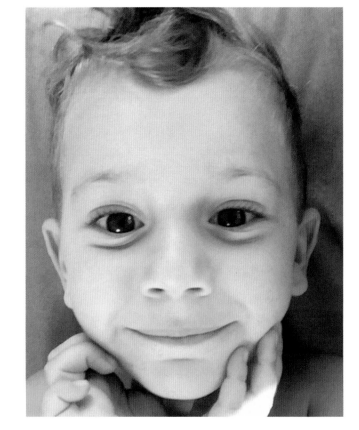

Family is important
to me. Starting a
relationship with
Brendan wasn't
a decision I took
lightly. But meeting
him (*top right*) and
his family showed
me how supportive
a partner and their
family could be.
Lahela and Noah
loved Brendan and
his family, but Ali
was still their dad.

The day Ali took Noah and Lahela to Beirut for a holiday I took a photo of Noah snuggled up with his dad. I was dreading being apart for two whole weeks, but I couldn't stop Ali from spending time with them and his family. If only!

Lahela and Noah's baby brother, Eli (*below left*). Eli and Brendan helped get me through my darkest days, but I can't wait until Eli gets to meet his brother and sister. And I get to hold them all close.

Arrested in Beirut. I'd been denied contact for months and I was desperate to see Lahela and Noah. I want them to know I tried everything and I never stopped wanting or trying to bring them home. So many lies have been told by others but the truth is, my estranged husband was supposed to have my children for two weeks and then they were to come home with me.

Before they went to Beirut I had some beautiful family photos taken. Now all I have are photos and memories, because Ali is still denying me access to our children. But I will be here, waiting, until Lahela and Noah come home.

A few seconds later, I was shoved out the door and into the back seat of a car several metres away. My dash alerted some more media outside, who began to scramble to get closer. Meanwhile, Tara had just begun her walk to our waiting vehicle. She reached the car only for her escorting officer to discover that it was locked. He banged on the door, and shouted at me to open it, but my hands were cuffed behind my back and the lock was some way away from me. Nevertheless I had to try, because the officer was frantic, and the media swarm actually looked quite scary. So, I shuffled forward on the seat – it's so much more difficult when you can't use your hands to push – and edged closer to the lock. Unfortunately, there were two rifles leaning against each other in front of me, and the closer I got to the lock, the closer I also was to staring down two barrels. As I leaned forward to have a go at the lock, I had only one obvious thought: *Please, don't go off!* I managed to half unlock the door, which was enough for it to be opened by a panicking officer who also reached for the lock, and banged my head with his body in the process. Moments later I turned to see Tara's head being shoved down by a hand to avoid it whacking the top of the car. Quick as a flash the door was shut, and Tara and I were inside while the media started to bang on the door.

'*Yalla! Yalla! Yalla!*' yelled the driver, and the car jolted away, with the two of us in the back seat thrown from side to side, while the media gave chase. It was all so dramatic, yet Tara was laughing.

'Are you all right?' I asked her.

'Well, that's going to make front-page news for us!'

It's weird the things that can go through your mind in an instant. Before we arrived back at the prison I imagined the news: Sally Faulkner shot in the head and killed by an unmanned police gun while she was trying to unlock a car door for Tara Brown. And then I thought about all the work the African women had put into making our hair look beautiful the day before.

And that was only the start of the craziness. Tara and I, still handcuffed, arrived back at prison to find two young men in clichéd white medical coats waiting for us.

'You need eye tests,' they said in English.

I looked at Tara with complete bewilderment.

'I'm sorry, but I already have glasses,' I told them.

That did nothing to convince them, so we were taken to the rooftop, where we sat and had our eyes examined. I wasn't sure about the methods used, because I spent most of the time looking from close range at my examiner's head, but at the end of it all, the examiner announced that I would have my prescription glasses in two weeks.

'Thank you, but I already have glasses. I don't have them with me right now, but I have some.'

I don't think he understood me, and he repeated that I would have my glasses soon. I shrugged my shoulders, and said, 'Whatever.' Then I looked at Tara.

'We *are* getting out of here, Tara. We are *not* going to be here in two weeks.'

'I hope so, Sally, I really hope so.'

I arrived back at Cell 3 to see two of the younger women sitting on a bed and tapping their toes to the sound of music coming from the TV. Before I walked through the door, a nun, complete with a habit and a cross around her neck, entered the cell and immediately stunned everyone. I, for one, must have looked surprised because Tara, who was at the door of her cell, asked what was up.

'There's a ninety-year-old nun in my cell dancing to Bollywood music!'

The nun invited me to dance with her. Don't ask me why, but I did, and all of a sudden others joined in. To this day I have no idea what I was thinking. I can only assume that I was so wound up that some part of my mind told me I needed a release, and to take it now. In that moment there was a fine line between the absurd and the very real, and I lost sense of both. Maybe I had snapped and this was my first step to true prison craziness. Most of us were dancing stupidly without a care in the world, and we didn't miss a step when the Bollywood music stopped and a Justin Bieber track came on – but then Mumma walked in. She frowned at us all, making sure we all knew she wasn't happy with this sort of behaviour in her cell. She reached for the remote control – which was always on her bed – and switched channels. And surprise, surprise, there was a news bulletin showing Tara being shoved, head down, into the police car. The nun quietly made her exit and I apologised to Mumma and sat down and watched the rest of the report.

But the bizarre hadn't finished yet. The next news story covered a ceremony for some women of Baabda prison who had graduated from their beauty practitioner's course. It showed pictures of the women, including the ones who had done our hair, receiving certificates in a presentation on the rooftop. Then, after that story, Ali's lawyer came up on screen in an interview. As I tried to make some sort of sense of what he was saying, Ketney decided she wanted me to teach her Aussie words that described cruel ex-husbands and bad boyfriends. I laughed.

'You don't have to say them, just write them down,' she said.

'Okay, but you have to try to pronounce them yourself.'

For the rest of the evening, I had a good laugh at hearing 'dickhead' and much worse coming from a particular top bunk.

Although it took my thoughts away from my predicament, it wasn't long before the cell quietened down and everyone tried to sleep – and I landed back into my nightmare. It happened early the next morning after I was again woken by the screams of the crying baby. They cut into me like a knife. Was there any way out? I worked myself up into a real state as I thought about the irony of the moment: here was a mother who was allowed to keep her baby with her in prison after murdering a child, and here was I separated from my children for doing what? I didn't sleep for the rest of the night, and by morning I was a wreck again.

Over the previous few days I had begun to write a letter, and that morning, I worked on it again. I'm not sure to whom I was really addressing it. Me? Lahela and Noah? Ali? The public? Judge Abdullah? Perhaps all of us. Or maybe none of us, and it was just a bit of self-imposed therapy. I scratched out a number of versions until I came up with this:

Whatever the outcome, I will accept and take grace in knowing I tried my best to be in my children's lives. My actions were simply an act of desperation that was forced by the position that my children and I were in. I would never wish this situation upon my worst enemy. When you love someone as much as I do Lahela and Noah, you would risk everything for them. I don't condone my actions. However, hearing my children cry for me, and hearing such sadness in their voices, broke me. Hearing them expressing how much they want to come home left me empty.

I'm sure there are thousands of parents who are in similar situations and can understand the emotions involved, and how no amount of tears will fix the emptiness. My actions were in the name of love. As long as my children know how much I love them, and that the destiny of their childhoods was taken out of my hands, then my actions weren't in vain. I'm sorry their voices weren't truly heard, and I'm sorry that some people find it so hard to understand that the children need both parents.

Neither Ali nor I are victims in all of this. The only ones I feel sorry for are our beautiful children. They deserve better than this. Our children's voices should be louder than all the other noise. Long after the media has forgotten this story, my children will still be living in a place they don't want to be without one of their parents. The saddest part is that it's been over eleven months now, and during this time my children have been denied their basic right to talk to their mother all because the laws facilitate this type of behaviour. Only when the laws change will we have happier children; unfortunately I have been trying to make this happen for almost a year without luck. I went through the legal system to gain full custody and was still denied my rights even after I was successful in the courts.

To Lahela and Noah, I'm sorry. Always remember Mummy loves you both so, so much, and no time apart will change that.

Ketney saw what I was doing, and asked if she could read the letter. Afterwards, she cried.

'I am praying for you,' she said. 'I would stay here twenty years more if it meant you could take your children back to Australia tomorrow. Twenty more years.'

Goodness in people is too precious to be measured.

After that, while still sitting on Ketney's bunk, I got a tap on my shoulder, and I turned to see Mumma.

'Nescafé?' she asked.

'No, thank you.'

She smiled, and blew me a kiss before returning to play cards with the woman who seemed to hate me.

Later, on the rooftop, Tara and I had our usual chat about best-case scenarios for us. It was then I first came to understand what 'an agreement' actually meant. Darren Wick had been meeting with the police and lawyers trying to negotiate to get us all out – and he knew that would mean compensation. However, Ali wasn't yet willing to 'agree' on a suitable sum of 'compensation'. Who knew what would happen next?

If an agreement was reached, it was likely all the *60 Minutes* crew and I would be released, but we could still face charges. At that stage, despite reports in the media, no charges had been laid. I wasn't aware of most media stories, but I knew enough to realise there was a lot of misinformation being spread. I could only rely on what I was being told by Ghassan, who had had his own unsuccessful negotiations with Ali's lawyer over the custody issue.

Apart from our brief passing along a corridor in the detention centre, I hadn't seen Adam or had the chance to speak with him. The only information I had about his court strategies and reactions was all second-hand. I'd heard that he'd said in the media that I was 'throwing everyone under the bus' to secure my own freedom. I was very upset by this, and I believe that the first cracks appeared in our relationship when Channel Nine began to deny it had paid CARI. I felt sorry for Adam because he was contracted to do a job that he believed was just and fair. We all did. He was helping me get my children home again. However, he knew the risks better than anyone, and I had to tell myself that above all else, no one forced him to do the job. It was his decision alone, and throughout the whole process I did everything the way he told me to. I still felt responsible, but this is what Adam did, this was his business. I had to let go of the guilt because I couldn't carry any more worries without breaking down completely.

My relationship with Nine's representatives, Darren Wick and Sallie Stone, had improved. By then, Sallie had apologised to me for the way she and Darren had practically ignored me the first few times I had seen them. Sallie told me they were both really affected by the situation and that Darren had been trying to do the right thing and not jeopardise anything. They'd both been briefed by the Channel Nine lawyers not to engage with me and had those words ringing in their ears when we first met. I accepted they had a job to do and were uncertain of how it was to be approached when they first arrived. The whole situation was fraught and I don't think anyone knew what to do or how to act. I remembered how I had lashed out at the police and the words I'd used when Lahela and Noah were taken from me again. There was no instruction manual for extreme situations like this. I accepted the apology.

Nevertheless, I was still wary of what might happen. It was all well and good to talk about agreements, but until one had actually been formalised, our only view of the world was through bars. And I was now kept from all three of my children.

Chapter Twenty-six

Embroidery was a popular pastime in prison. Not only did it give the women something to do, it was a way to earn money for food and other necessities. Participants would be given cotton, needles, sequins, beads and material that could be turned into sparkling patches for handbags or artworks. The final products were taken outside by a woman who conducted bible sessions on the rooftop every Sunday, and given to people to sell on our behalf. The bible lady would bring all the money raised back to the makers in what was quite a successful little business. Although I didn't want to become involved, because I didn't want to think I'd be in the prison very long, I did partake in an offshoot where leftover beads were used to make bracelets. Ketney and some of the African women were very adept at this, and with some instruction from my cellmates I soon got the hang of making my own pieces. I was working on one with 'Mummy loves Lala' (Lahela) when I found out Tara and I would be going back to Judge Abdullah on Wednesday, 20 April.

Despite 'agreement' talk, I was anything but confident when we arrived at the detention centre. Ghassan had told me little about what was happening; I accepted he had his reasons for being tight-lipped. As opposed to previous appearances, Tara and I were kept waiting in an open hall-like area near Judge Abdullah's office. One police officer, with a distinct shaven head and bushy eyebrows, walked up to us. We had seen him on our previous trips, and he always acknowledged us with a stern: 'Are you good?' This day was no different. We nodded and said, 'Yes.' As he walked away, another officer came over to us. He must have seen how nervous we were. I was taking deep breaths, and Tara was tapping her slipper-like shoes on the floor.

'It's all right, you go home, you go home,' he said.

And then he winked at us, and also walked away.

I looked at Tara and said: 'I'll believe that when I hear the judge say it.'

'So will I.'

Before I could focus too much on what the officer had said, two low, bellowing voices interrupted my thoughts. I looked up to see two more officers ready to escort us into the judge's office. My stomach churned as we walked in to see Judge Abdullah, our lawyers, the interpreter I disliked, the transcriber and a few other officers. Ali was there too, and I was stopped only a step or two away from him; I was so close I could smell his cologne. Thankfully Ghassan stood between us. The small room became even more crowded after the door opened and Stephen, Ben and Tangles were brought in. It was the first time I had seen them since we were all in the detention-centre cells. The guys had remained in the centre for the entire time, and they now all wore beards. We greeted each other as they were guided in behind Tara and me. Tangles was especially keen to find out how we were. Their presence lifted me, and I knew that the appearance of us all together in front of Judge Abdullah meant this was not going to be another question-and-answer session.

Judge Abdullah stood up behind his desk and announced that an agreement had been made. As he said that, I noticed a pile of paperwork in front of Ali, who was standing to the side of the same desk. And on the top of that paperwork was a photocopy of a cheque with a line through it. It was there as clear as day. It was then that I realised the 'agreement' was indeed to do with a payment being made. I couldn't see the amount, but at that moment, it didn't matter. I felt so angry. Was this what this was all about – money? Is that why the *60 Minutes* crew and I had been in prison? And why Adam and his workers still were? All the pieces came together in that instant. Money. Ali was after money. And Channel Nine had been forced to give it to him to get us out.

My attention returned to Judge Abdullah, who announced that we were all to be released from prison and were free to return to Australia. I began to shake with relief. I looked at Tara who was blank-faced, but when she looked at me she raised a little smile. I turned to see Ben ease his head back and sigh. Tangles let out a big rush of air as well. Stephen's expression was like Tara's.

At the request of Judge Abdullah and on the advice of our respective lawyers, we had to sign papers to acknowledge we consented to the agreement, which I still didn't have the details of.

Judge Abdullah also said Ali wanted to address me, but before that happened, Ali did something else that dumbfounded every single one of us who heard him. He looked at Ben and said: 'Do you want to go for a surf later? You look like one of my buddies I go surfing with.'

What could we say to that? Poor Ben stood there speechless, and Tara rolled her eyes and quietly scoffed.

'That's the only reason, buddy, why you guys got off. Because you look like one of the guys I surf with.'

I then heard Ali say, 'Fuckin' dickheads,' under his breath.

Ali's only act of any goodwill was his acceptance that we should all have our handcuffs removed. However, I still had one cuff hanging from my wrist when Judge Abdullah told me Ali wanted to address me individually. I sat at the desk and waited, dreading what might happen.

'Sal, you're not going anywhere. You're staying here for two more days.'

I stiffened. Tara put a hand on my shoulder to try to comfort me.

'What do you mean?' I asked.

'You have to sign paperwork. I want you to sign over your parental rights. You're going to give me sole custody of the children, and I want you to revoke their Australian citizenship, so I can get them American passports.'

I burst into tears. 'You can't stop them being Australian citizens. They were born there! And I can't revoke the Australian custody. They are court orders. What are you trying to do, Ali?'

Now I felt Tara shaking, but I sensed it was with anger. But what did Ali care? His eyes were as cold as they had ever been, and they were telling me: *You're nothing, and you'll do as I say.* At about this point the Channel Nine lawyer threw his hands in the air and stormed out, saying he was disgusted and didn't want anything to do with what was happening. Ghassan, however, began to protest: 'Stop, stop. You cannot do this.' Judge Abdullah then stepped in and lectured Ali.

'You cannot make those demands here. Sally is their mother. She doesn't have to do anything you have just said.'

Those words calmed me a little, and I pushed myself higher in my chair. My eyes burned, as they nearly always did.

'Okay,' acknowledged Ali, obviously not wanting to show disrespect to the judge. 'We'll talk about that later.'

I had to sign the agreement the lawyers had thrashed out and I was distraught when I discovered they did give custody to Ali in Lebanon, but I consoled myself with the fact I was in no way relinquishing my rights. Ali had shown me that Lebanese law operated separately to Australian law, so I didn't believe that an agreement signed under duress would mean anything in an Australian court. I couldn't stay in prison, he wasn't allowing me to see Lahela and Noah, so I had to get home to Eli and then work out what to do next. I wasn't going to give up the fight.

Judge Abdullah asked Ali if there was anything else he wanted to say.

'If you want to see the kids, you can see them tomorrow. I'll bring them here and you can spend some time with them. Maybe we can get a bite to eat or get some lunch or something.'

'I don't want to have lunch with you, Ali. In all honesty I struggle to be in the same room as you. I will come here to see the children, but not you.'

My response didn't seem to bother him at all. Before he left with his lawyer he agreed I could see the children in a play centre or park. Judge Abdullah stepped in to say that we were first to come to his office at 10.30 in the morning. And that was about the end of it.

We walked out of the office, along a hallway and into a room where Maggie, Pascal, Darren Wick and Sallie Stone were waiting. Maggie was already in frenetic organising mode, while Pascal trailed behind her taking notes with a pen and notebook. We were all relieved, but it wasn't a time for any type of celebration, especially when Tara told everyone I couldn't yet leave Lebanon. Sallie Stone, who was very keen to get everyone on a plane, decided she would stay behind with me.

While Maggie finalised transport details, Tara and I endured one final trip back to the prison in the old truck. The media of course snapped away and fired questions at us. As we bounced along, no longer handcuffed, we stood up, hugged, lost our balance and laughed. And we cried too.

'I can't believe we're out,' I said.

We sat back down and smiled at each other.

'Oh, I don't have to sleep in those beds anymore. And we don't have to kill any more spiders,' said Tara.

My overriding thought was about freedom, but I also knew as we hurried past the media back into the prison that I wasn't yet free.

And perhaps I never would be. Lahela and Noah were still with Ali, and his cold eyes gave me no hope that he would let me see them.

Chapter Twenty-seven

A clean, soft bed; a shower; decent food. It had been too long. I was in the house of Glenn Miles, the Australian Ambassador to Lebanon. The previous few hours had rushed by in such a blur that my thoughts were only beginning to catch up with all that had happened.

First, the goodbyes in Cell 3. Everyone – apart from the woman who disliked me, and the other who barely moved – hugged me and wished me well. Ketney was in tears.

'This is why I don't make friends here. I make good friends with you, and now you go and I'm lonely again.'

She promised she would finish the bracelet I had been working on. I thanked her and left. I then gave prison authorities $US50 to pass on to the cell for food.

Then, Tara and I were bundled into a van outside the prison, where the media pack was the most aggressive yet. The vehicle was banged and I actually felt as though it was swaying from side to side even before we'd driven off. Poor Maggie, who tried to conduct the exercise with military precision, had her glasses knocked off. Inside the van, the *60 Minutes* guys were waiting. We all hugged and smiled. And then the laughter came. Ben, who had a huge bulky old camera that had been found from who knows where, filmed some footage and short interviews. I was happy, yet my overriding need was to apologise. I felt terribly guilty that I had taken Stephen, Tara, Ben and Tangles away from their loved ones and precious family lives. They too had suffered greatly because of what they had left behind. Tangles could see I was right on the edge and asked if I was okay. I started to cry.

'I'm sorry,' I said. 'I wanted to say sorry in the judge's office after we were told we were being released, but I knew I'd just start crying there as well.'

'Don't be sorry. We are sorry. You don't have your children.'

Tara supported Tangles: 'Sally, you're the one who has lost out. Don't ever feel the need to apologise to us.'

I felt somewhat reassured by their words, but there was also a heavy cloud of doubt in my thoughts. The *60 Minutes* guys were on their way to the airport to go home, but I was staying behind. I was also concerned about Adam and his team. I hated to think of them left in the jail. I worried about Mohammed and about his parents. I should have been so excited about the prospect of seeing Lahela and Noah again, but at that moment it was only a prospect, and I tormented myself by wondering what stunts Ali might yet pull.

Maggie gave me her phone so I could ring Brendan. I was so desperate to hear his voice that each ring felt like a minute. Finally, he answered. His voice was a little croaky; I'd woken him up. At first, he didn't recognise me, but then suddenly, there was a rush of emotion and I could feel his tears from thousands of miles away.

'Oh my God, Sally! Are you okay? Oh my God, I can't believe you're out. You don't know how good it is to hear your voice.'

He said Eli was asleep next to him, and all was well. It was such a simple, yet beautiful thing to say. I told him I had to stay for a few more days. He was concerned, but after all he'd been through, he could wait.

The airport farewells with the *60 Minutes* guys were low-key. There were more hugs and assurances that we would all get together soon. Then, I was taken to the ambassador's house. Until I left Lebanon, I had to be escorted by an Australian embassy official everywhere in public. But now, in the quiet of my temporary bedroom, I was alone. I hadn't been by myself for two weeks. I'm unable to adequately describe in these pages how I felt at that time. Yes, it was strange, but beyond that . . . well, there was a hollowness that ached, yet a feeling of utter relief. Was it wrong of me to feel some sense of happiness? I knew I was screwed up. And knowing that alone made me feel more screwed up. As I say, I cannot adequately describe it.

Not long after I arrived at Ambassador Miles' house I saw a copy of *The Australian* newspaper that had a picture of Tara and me on the front page. The ambassador's wife caught me looking at it, and cheerfully made light of it and folded it away behind the breakfast bar. It was just one of those little moments that reminded me how real my situation was. But if I thought I knew all there was to know about what had happened, it took only a phone call to my mum to change that.

She told me how the whole family, including Brendan and Eli, had been put up in a hotel by *60 Minutes* to be sheltered from the rest of the media.

'We've had camera crews and photographers out the front of the house for days,' said Mum.

Both Brendan and my brother Simon were going to work from the hotel each day. One afternoon Simon needed to return to Mum's house to pick up some bits and pieces, but he was so hassled by the media knocking on the door and waiting at the end of the driveway that he rang Mum and said: 'I'm over this! I can't even get out. They're standing right behind my car.' *60 Minutes*' Executive Producer, Kirsty Thomson, was soon on the phone advising him not to say anything to anyone. She warned him not to go to the hotel, because there was a chance he would be followed, but he was so angry he told her he was tired and needed to sleep, and then he hung up on her.

Mum also told me that some of my friends had been harassed, and even my uncle who was visiting from the United States for a fortnight had received phone calls. Hearing all of that added to my guilt. I tried to calm Mum down, but I only made things worse when I said that I wasn't yet coming home. She immediately clicked into extreme-worry mode; like me, she was concerned what Ali might do. I assured her I didn't think anything would happen, and the delay was all to do with me spending time with Lahela and Noah. However, I did not wholly believe that assurance myself.

I could do nothing but wait.

And hope.

The next morning, I woke early and looked at the time; 10.30 couldn't come soon enough. I have rarely been more grateful to have someone with me than I was to have Maggie as we drove to the detention centre for what I hoped would be the final time. We pulled up to the now predictable media scrum, but this time I was sensitive to what was happening. I picked up the voices of Australians tossing questions at me through the craziness: 'What does it feel like to be released?'

'How do you feel about seeing your children again?' 'When are you going to leave?'

We walked into Judge Abdullah's office. Ali came in moments later, but my heart sank when I couldn't see Lahela and Noah. Ali gave me a little nod and a half-smile. Judge Abdullah explained to me that Ali thought it was best for the kids to avoid the media, and they would instead be waiting at a playground. I agreed. I didn't want them stressed either.

'Are you sure I'm going to see them?' I asked Ali.

'Yeah, no worries.'

We arranged a time, and then I went with Ghassan and Sallie Stone to the office of the handsome commander who had continued to turn heads throughout the whole ordeal. We walked in, and the first thing I noticed was a brand-new coffee machine sitting on a bench. The commander was very happily sipping from a cup.

'Good machine, good coffee,' he said proudly.

I looked at Sallie, who confirmed what I was already thinking: the machine was a gift from Channel Nine. By then, all the tension of the previous fortnight seemed forgotten, and we were all suddenly friends. Sallie even asked the commander for a selfie. He was a little reluctant at first, but then he realised he was the commander and could do as he liked. He stood up, puffed out his chest and posed proudly. Sallie thanked him, and he patted her shoulder before walking back behind his desk and sitting down.

Another officer walked in and said something in Arabic to the commander, and within seconds the commander had opened a stylish case full of coffee pods. It is so ridiculously surreal to think my last distinct memory of being in the detention centre is one of the commander pressing a button and a coffee machine hissing back at him.

We left the building, and although I had been advised not to engage the media pack, I felt compelled to speak as I walked to the car: 'All I can say is that I love my children, and I did it because I love my children.'

And it was now time to show them that love in person.

I was nervous. I was excited. And I was also very, very sad.

Chapter Twenty-eight

The advice from the embassy wasn't what I wanted to hear.

'I suggest you leave for Australia today,' said Maggie.

She had checked Lebanon's airport watchlist, and my name wasn't on it. Considering all that had happened, though, there were no guarantees that things wouldn't change in a heartbeat. Certainly, I knew I couldn't trust Ali. He'd more than shown me that his promises didn't mean anything. But in leaving Lebanon, I would also have no choice but to leave behind Lahela and Noah. I already knew that would happen, but it was only now, on what was going to be my last day in the country, that the brutality of that knowledge was starting to smash me to pieces. By leaving the children, I would be acknowledging that Ali would have custody of Lahela and Noah for the foreseeable future, and perhaps forever.

Forever.

The thought crushed me.

Now, I sat waiting in an embassy car for the chance to say both hello and goodbye to my children. Maggie and Pascal were with me, and as they made arrangements to change my airline ticket, I stared out the window at the McDonald's restaurant and play centre where Ali had arranged to meet me. Before too long, a white four-wheel-drive Toyota pulled up near us, and a stocky man with dark rings under his eyes got out. He was carrying a satchel. We looked at each other, and I froze. He looked hard and a bit scary. I immediately thought he had a connection with Ali, and I waited for the next arrival. Sure enough, Ali pulled up in a car driven by his friend Mustafa. His cousin, Derek, came next in a different car with Lahela and Noah.

I sat at a table near the playground and waited for Ali to approach me.

'Listen,' he said. 'I don't want you to cry at all in front of the kids. If you do, we're leaving. I want this to be a happy time. I don't want you getting emotional.'

'I understand, but I'm not a robot either. I'll try, but I can't promise you.'

'Well, that's how it is. If you cry, we leave. And you're not to take photos of the kids either.'

'What? What the hell, Ali, they're my kids too.'

We argued until it was decided I could take pictures, but only on Ali's phone. He promised he would then send through the photos later. I doubted he would do it, but now wasn't the time to push him.

'All right then, go and get them,' he said.

'What?'

'Go and get the kids.'

I walked over to Derek's car where Lahela and Noah were still strapped in. As I looked through the window, they were talking to each other and swinging their legs. I opened the door and they both stopped and looked at me. Lahela smiled shyly and put her arms out; Noah said matter-of-factly: 'Hi, Mum.'

'Do you guys want to play?' I asked them.

'Yeah! Yeah!' said Lahela.

I wanted to burst into tears of happiness, but I couldn't cry, I didn't want to give any excuse for Ali to cut our time together short. I blinked a few times and tried my best to dry my eyes as I helped them get out of the car. Lahela was so excited, but Noah went quiet, and he let go of my hand. After he got out, he stared at me and didn't move.

'You can go back to Daddy if you want to,' I told him.

Lahela encouraged him but he wouldn't be swayed.

'Daddy! Daddy!'

Ali picked Noah up and held him while Lahela and I went to the playground. Our three-year-old son watched from several metres away for fifteen minutes. Then, without any fuss, he came across and grabbed my hand. I felt a wave of warmth.

'Can I have a cuddle?' I asked him.

He put out his hands and gave me a huge hug. Lahela stopped playing on some equipment and rushed over to join us. We were in the middle of a walkway and people had to move around us, but I didn't care. Nor did I ever want to let go.

'Mummy loves you both so much. I'm so sorry that you don't get to come back with me.'

'Will we get to see you again soon, Mummy?' asked Lahela.

It was a question I couldn't bring myself to answer. The truth was, I didn't know. Instead, I told her it was time for a 'big play'. In the minutes that followed I wished I had the power to stop time. I was absorbed in watching my children's every move and hearing their every sound. I filmed them climbing through a tube and hiding from me.

'Noah, Lahela, where are you?'

'Over here, Mum.'

Just to hear that one word. Just to hear *Mum*. What mother wouldn't be swept away in the moment?

'Noah, guess what?'

'What?'

'I love you.'

'I love you too.'

'Lahela, guess what?'

'What?'

'I love you.'

'I love you too, Mummy.'

I followed them round in the tube. Lahela stopped and turned towards me.

'Do you want to sing me the Mummy song?' I asked her.

Lahela broke into the Mother's Day song, the same one that she'd sung in the safe house.

'*Mummy, I love you so much when you are here . . .*'

She couldn't remember all the words, so she made up lines as she went along. She didn't miss a beat. It was so beautiful, the type of moment a parent might hold onto long after their child's innocence has gone. I told her I loved her all the time and then Noah wanted to keep moving. I wanted time to stop so I could stay with them. When I looked over, I saw Ali watching us, emotionless, standing next to Derek, Mustafa and the tough man in the playground's entrance.

The children and I moved to another part of the play-ground. Noah was struggling to put his shoes back on, so I began to help him. Ali came over and said: 'He can do that himself.'

'This is my time with them, Ali. Let me put them on, please.'

Ali moved away, and I caught the eye of his cousin.

'Are you okay?' mouthed Derek.

I nodded. I knew Derek reasonably well. On a previous trip to Lebanon he had stayed with Ali and me in the apartment, and I had cooked all his food and done his washing. If only he could now repay me by convincing Ali to soften his approach, to even change his mind over custody. But that wasn't going to happen.

After forty-five minutes, Ali said it was time to go.

'But it hasn't even been an hour,' I protested.

'Nah, I've got to go. I've got a meeting with a client.'

'I want to go with Mummy,' pleaded Lahela.

'No, baby. You're going to come with Daddy. Daddy has to go to work.'

'You got to go to work?' asked Noah. 'You're going to leave us again?'

I felt a rush of sadness and implored Ali to at least take the kids to work with him. He agreed, but Lahela didn't want to move. I bent down and told her how much I loved her. Now, there was no chance of me holding back the tears.

'Why are you sad, Mummy?'

'I'm not sad, sweetheart. I'm happy because I got to spend time with you and Noah.'

Lahela turned and looked at Ali.

'Can Mummy come back to our house so we can paint our nails together?'

Ali ignored her, and hurried them up. Lahela stopped for a moment and told me she had a surprise for me.

'Oh, great. When do I get it?'

'In a minute.'

I took Lahela and Noah to Derek's car, and kneeled down and hugged them together for the final time. I strapped Noah into his seat, and kissed his forehead. He smiled in his half-smile kind of way, and squirmed and kicked. I walked around the other side of the car to strap Lahela in.

'Wait on, Mummy.'

She took a pink plastic ring off one of her fingers. It was shaped in a love heart.

'This is my favourite ring. You can have it so you don't forget me.'

'Mummy will never forget you. Why would you think that?'

'Because I'm not seeing you again.'

Lahela knew only too well what was going on. I say again, she was – and I have no doubt she still is – an old soul.

By then, Ali was behind me next to the door.

'Lahela gave me this ring,' I said.

'Cute.'

I stepped back and looked at the children. My last memory is of Lahela smiling. And then Ali shut the door.

'This is so wrong, Ali. I'll never understand why you've done this.'

'Look, we'll talk,' he said. 'You'll get to see the kids. I'll make sure you can Skype them.'

'Promise?'

'Yeah, I promise.'

Derek drove off, and I could no longer restrain myself. My knees buckled and I cried and cried and cried. My precious children had gone. I had failed. And my acknowledgment of that failure was now on display for the man who had shown me many times he thrived on seeing me defeated. Ali grabbed me and held me tight. I was too weak to resist.

'Ssh,' he said. 'It's okay. Sal, you know why I did this?'

I held my breath.

'Sal, I did this because I still love you.'

I found the strength to push Ali away.

'What did you just say?' I whispered.

'I did this because I still love you. I just needed space.'

I'd gone nearly a whole year without seeing my kids. Then two weeks in jail. And now Ali was telling me he loved me. I felt crazy with anger.

'You are sick. *You are sick!* Oh my God. How can you say that? How?'

Ali stood there. He gave nothing. And I had nothing to give.

'Send me a message tomorrow, and maybe we can catch up again if you want to see the kids.'

I turned away from him and walked back to Maggie and Pascal, who were waiting at a park bench.

We drove to the Australian embassy, and by the time we arrived, there was only one thing I could do. I ran from Maggie's office, found a toilet, and threw up. By the time I returned to the office I could barely keep my eyes open. I fell asleep on a couch, and woke up to the sounds of the evening calls to prayer, and the spread of a red sunset across the city.

Part IV

Part IV

Chapter Twenty-nine

Sallie Stone, bless her, held my hand as we walked through a back door of Sydney airport and into a van that had been arranged by *60 Minutes*. We escaped the waiting media scrum and were taken to the Stamford Hotel in the city, where my family, having been flown from Brisbane, was waiting in a suite, complete with camera operators and producers to film the reunion.

It was Friday, 22 April 2016.

Obviously, it was all very emotional. When I held gorgeous Eli, I cried – but the tears weren't only because I had my baby; they were also for the children I had left behind. When I hugged Brendan I felt as though no one in the world needed more reassurance than he did. He too had been left behind, although in a very different way. I apologised to everyone for dragging them all down.

Later, Tara arrived. It was wonderful to see her. She said she'd sat down with her two boys, Jack and Tom, and told them what had happened. They'd been protected from the daily news by their father and had no idea of their mum's ordeal. But it seemed neither of them was overly fussed by their mum's explanation, until Tara mentioned she had been in jail. Cool! Tara and I laughed about that. We promised we would keep in touch, and have done so.

Late that night we were taken to another Sydney hotel, where my family was staying. Holding Eli gave me some comfort and I was relieved that after all that had happened and having been away from him for so long, I was still able to breastfeed. At least that connection hadn't been broken. At night I couldn't sleep, and over the following days I was very restless. Voices mashed together in my head in one indecipherable mass of white noise. Whether I was asleep or awake I leaped at even the slightest unexpected sound; a mere tap on the door was enough to sit me bolt upright. I tossed and turned over disturbing family revelations to which I had been oblivious in my prison cell.

One of the worst stories involved my father, who knew nothing about the recovery plans when I went to Beirut. It wasn't long after the recovery happened that Dad received a phone call from one of Ali's friends who lived on the Gold

Coast; he informed Dad that Ali had rung him with the news that Lahela and Noah had been taken off the street by men with guns. I could only imagine how furious and worried Dad would have been. He soon put two and two together and drove to Mum's place and virtually knocked down the door on his way to having a heated argument with Brendan and Mum. It ended when Mum told Dad to get out and she slammed the door behind him.

Poor Brendan had copped more than anyone. His phone had rung endlessly with media requests and queries. A top-rating radio show offered him $3000 for an exclusive, but he had no intention of giving any interviews. A few days after my return he received a call from a journalist who asked if he had punched Ali in the head during a fight, which was ridiculous; they had never even met.

I was really fidgety and tense, and Brendan suggested I seek professional counselling and perhaps take some sort of medication. It was sensible advice but it grated on me because I thought he was saying I was weak. Brendan then tried to hug me, but I shoved him, hard.

'What *is* your problem?' he said.

I apologised to Brendan, who had steadfastly supported me while I tried to get Lahela and Noah back.

Brendan had tears in his eyes. He picked up Eli and walked out of the room, and didn't come back for quite some time. I think I was waiting for him to punish me, to shut me out and treat me coldly. It was what I had grown used to in my marriage – but Brendan never did any of that. He never played emotional games and I always knew where I stood. I was dozing on the bed when he returned.

'I'm sorry,' he said. 'I thought you were gone. I thought I was going to be a single dad. I didn't know what I was going to do. Thank God for my parents and your mum.'

We hugged and cried together. He revealed that there was one day when he sat at his computer writing emails, watching news reports, waiting and hoping. He wouldn't leave his chair. Eventually his father drove up from the Gold Coast and told him he had to get away from it. Then, he broke down.

'I really don't know what you went through over there, Sally. But you have to know, it was hell back here too. I didn't want to let Eli out of my sight. I didn't put him in his cot, so he slept next to me on the bed. I kept telling him every night, "Mummy's coming home soon."'

Brendan then shook his head and insisted that despite all he had gone through, he would support me if I had to do it all over again. Now, as I reflect on that moment, I am humbled to know I have such a strong and loving man in my life.

After a week in the hotel, we all decided it was time to get home and take a step back into our everyday lives.

Back in Brisbane, I battened down at Mum's place. When I did go out, I got the occasional sideways glance from people,

and on one occasion I was about to grab some frozen peas
– of all things – in a grocery market when a woman hugged
me and cried. By then, *60 Minutes* had broadcast a story
about the recovery and our homecoming. For legal reasons,
there was much that couldn't be said or shown, and at the
time of writing this book, I have no idea whether Channel
Nine will ever show another story.

Whether or not it was wise to do so, in the weeks after
my return I sifted through media reports about the recovery,
the court proceedings and my time in prison. These reports
opened my eyes to the impact the story had in Australia, or
at least in the media. Prime Minister Malcolm Turnbull and
Opposition Leader Bill Shorten both commented; talkback
radio had whipped it up; social media was huge; and I gather
there would have been more than a few pub conversations
about it. Brendan could certainly vouch for that; when the
recovery first hit the news, none of Brendan's workmates
knew that I was his partner, but after a while – and after
having to listen to many comments from others – he revealed
all, much to everyone's shock.

Some media reports were close to the mark; others were
so far away from it that I can only assume the material was
made up. I accept that the media was attempting to do its
job in some trying conditions, but I will state that I never
gave up custody of my children in Australia, and the orders
of the Family Court still stand. If Ali ever wants to come

and dispute that, I would be happy to see him in court. And there are two reports that I feel I must comment on.

On 21 April 2016, the day after the *60 Minutes* crew and I were released, Sydney radio station KIIS 1065 ran an interview with Ali on the Kyle and Jackie O show in which Ali said the reason he kept Lahela and Noah was because he didn't like my parenting style. He based his argument on Lahela's apparent complaint that 'Mummy's friend' (Brendan) slept in the same bed as Lahela and Noah. Ali added that he 'wasn't okay with all of that'. It never happened. Yes, Brendan sat on their beds and played 'aeroplanes' with them and sometimes stayed in their room with me while I read to them until they fell asleep. But that was all. Nothing else. He *never* slept in their bed with them. However, I do acknowledge that Ali wasn't at all happy about Brendan's presence in our children's lives. He had suggested a couple of times that I should not see Brendan when the children were present. I respected Ali's parental requests in every other way, but I refused to be dictated to by Ali on this. Brendan is a very good man, and Ali was insinuating otherwise. It made me angry. I was doing nothing wrong or inappropriate. He had asked me for a divorce and we both knew that was the right thing for us. I was moving on with my life, and such was the happy relationship that Brendan and the children had, I saw no harm in them knowing him.

I had no idea the level of anger that was festering in Ali about this issue or that he would use this to justify taking the children from me. I only learned about it in one of our Skype calls when he verbally attacked me about Brendan hugging me in front of Lahela. He said, 'Fuck, what were you teaching her?' By then, my relationship with Ali was dead. At the time of writing, our divorce is still to happen, but I guarantee it will.

Ali also said in the radio interview that he cut off contact between the kids and me because he saw that I was 'trying to orchestrate a kidnapping'. I find that even more disturbing. I was never kidnapping my children. Their father had taken them from me and refused to send them home.

If what he says is true about knowing that I was planning to come to Beirut to reclaim our children ten months after he cut off contact, the big question, for which I have no definitive answer, is: How did he know? He confirmed that he had seen email exchanges between recovery agents and me on the iPad I had given Lahela and Noah. When Ali refused to send the kids home from Lebanon, I did search for ways to see them and I researched my legal options, but how could he access my email account without me knowing?

After my very first discussion with recovery agent Col Chapman I thought it was wise to change my email address, so I opened a new account that Ali couldn't possibly have known about. From my memory, there was only one possible piece of correspondence concerning recovery operations that Ali might have been able to access through my old email address: a scanned article about parental alienation that Col Chapman sent me. After reading it, I put the article into my email's trash. Did Ali sift through my trash? And even if he did, it's an extraordinary leap from reading one preliminary article about parental alienation to knowing when a recovery operation being undertaken by *another* agent was actually going to take place. So, if Ali did see relevant emails, *how* did he get them? And *who* provided him with my new address details and *how* did he break through a double-security password without my knowledge? I only started to interact with the media and contact recovery agents *after* Ali told me Lahela and Noah weren't coming back to Australia.

Furthermore, Ali said that I was using Skype to 'pinpoint' every move that he made with Lahela and Noah, and that it was this that prompted him to say he couldn't 'communicate' with me anymore. I don't really know why Ali stopped my communication with the children, but he did say it was because the kids were always upset whenever they spoke with me.

Well, yes, they were upset. They wanted to come home. They wanted their mum. I recorded a number of Skype conversations with Ali during this period in which he told me this; I cling to those recordings now because it allows me to hear the children's voices. But they also break my heart because of the sadness they convey. To hear Lahela telling me with such a fragile voice that she wants to come back to Australia is so distressing that I only listen to the recordings when I am at my strongest.

Ali also said during this interview that he had tried to move to Australia a 'bunch of times'. If that is true, I never stopped him.

Finally, he said the arrests and subsequent court proceedings were 'all about the custody of the kids', and when asked if he received any payment he replied, 'Negative.' This is blatantly untrue. Ali and also his mother were paid; it is as simple as that and it cannot be truthfully denied. I do not know the amount, but I can say with assuredness that Ali *did receive payment*.

Ali used the word 'negative' again concerning the payment question when he was interviewed on *The Project* on Channel Ten. In this interview he said that I contacted him in April 2015 and said that Noah wanted to live in Lebanon. I did not say that. I have *never* said that. I did tell Ali that Noah was missing him, and I asked Ali when he was next likely to come to Australia. When he was away from the children for three months at a time, both Lahela and Noah would miss him. The day in question – or the day Ali suggests I said that Noah wanted to move to Lebanon – followed a massive session that the children had at Chipmunks. The kids were very tired and Noah had a meltdown at bedtime and kept saying: 'I want Daddy!' That hit me hard, so, after the children were asleep I contacted Ali on WhatsApp and asked him if I could Skype-call him. He said he was at the beach but could find time to talk. When we did, he told me he hoped to come back to Australia soon. As it turned out, his next visit was when he looked after the kids while I did my science prac work in Rockhampton.

Ali also said in that television interview: 'I told her from day one. I never told her she can't see the kids.' Wrong. I had all too many Skype conversations in which Ali said exactly the opposite. In the interview he also said that the time difference between Australia and Lebanon helped him explain to Lahela and Noah why they couldn't talk with me on Skype; he implied that when it is night in Lebanon it is daytime in Australia. There is seven hours' difference between Australia's Eastern Standard time and Lebanon's time. So, for example, 7am in Brisbane is 2pm in Beirut. Daylight at both ends. More than enough time for me to talk to the children without disturbing sleep for any of us. Ali's excuse holds no weight.

I can't help feeling that Ali is slowly brainwashing the kids against me, slowly removing me from their lives, one sentence at a time. That is what parental alienation is – it is what so many other mothers, fathers, grandparents and extended family have to live with. I need Lahela and Noah to know that I would call, Skype or visit in a heartbeat if their father would allow me to and the possibility of being jailed wasn't an issue. As I have said before, at this moment, Ali has all the power and he is using it to keep Lahela and Noah away from me.

It has been very distressing to hear recently that Ali is starting to spread vicious rumours about me. What he is claiming is beyond awful and though every word is untrue, he doesn't seem to care. I don't understand why he would do this – but I won't allow his slander and defamation to go unchallenged. I am terrified that Lahela and Noah will be told awful things about me. I need them to know none of it is true.

The most disturbing part of *The Project* interview was Ali's failure to adequately answer the question: 'If you knew about this [the recovery attempt] ahead of time, why not stop it before your kids had to go through that trauma?' He said that he expected me to go and speak with him after the Tuesday attempt – the day Ali escorted Lahela and Noah to school – was aborted. I had been trying to contact Ali for months and months without success, and by then, I was desperate.

If Ali did know about the recovery operation, did he plan for my arrest? Hope for it? In one of our text-message conversations before he cut contact, Ali had railed at the description of him as a kidnapper. He angrily told me that the kids were with their father, so it wasn't kidnapping. He believes it was okay for him to go against Australian Family Court custody orders and refuse to bring them back. Well,

I didn't kidnap our children. I had full custody and was being denied access. I was in Lebanon reclaiming my rights.

I tortured myself reading through those initial reports, and since then I have been very upset by some other happenings in the media. Most recently Channel Nine's *Today* show ran a 'Hello World' holiday promotion that included photos of Lahela and Noah to advertise a joyful holiday. Someone must have discovered the picture of my gorgeous children and didn't realise who they were, but it was still wrong. I also learned that during my imprisonment in Beirut the Nine MSN website ran a picture of the children and me with a caption that wrongly identified us as a family that had been murdered. And *Woman's Day* magazine ran a story that lifted pictures and text from my Instagram page without permission.

I have seen many hurtful comments about me online, and I try to ignore them. I know the truth of my story. And even after all that Ali has done, I don't want others to attack him or to abuse him on social media because I don't want my children to ever be exposed to that kind of hate. What Ali has done is wrong, but keyboard hate is not going to help bring Lahela and Noah home.

Such examples have taught me much about the media. Things I wish I didn't know. On the flip side, I have been treated fairly by many other organisations. And I did use the media to try to get Lahela and Noah home, so I realise some will say I brought it all on myself. I assume the mix of good and bad will always happen.

Only days before this book went to the printer, I watched an interview Adam Whittington did on Channel Seven's *Sunday Night* program. It would be an understatement to say things had been tense since the *60 Minutes* crew and I were released and Adam remained in custody, and any communications since his release have been fraught.

It was horrific to see Adam's tears when asked about his time in jail and to hear the pain in his voice as he talked about missing his children. I know that pain. I learned in that interview where Adam was arrested but I still don't know exactly how things fell apart. It was revealed Adam had filmed an interview onboard the getaway boat the night before the recovery, in which he mentioned a big story he was doing with *60 Minutes*. I am not sure if this was for a documentary or a news program, but I hope it wasn't a factor in everything turning bad. Going from what Ali told me that first day after I was arrested, it wasn't.

The *Sunday Night* interview suggested my Facebook posts were the reason we were caught, but this is not true. There are also things Adam stated during the interview that aren't correct.

He said that when I first contacted him in 2015 to learn about how child recovery works he instructed me to get formal custody in Australia so he could help me, but he didn't tell me this. I was already in the process of formalising custody arrangements in the Family Court well before I spoke to Adam. And in 2016, contrary to Adam telling the program I commissioned him to carry out the recovery, his involvement, as far as I knew, rolled over from the initial negotiations between the freelance journalist who pitched my story to Channel Seven, with CARI attached.

What really confused me in the *Sunday Night* interview was when Adam relayed step by step what had happened during the actual recovery of the children. Using the grainy CCTV footage he explained who was where and then pointed out that I had picked up one of the children. This isn't what happened, but Adam wasn't there so it is understandable he got that wrong. He'd hired other people to do the job. However, he was right when he said no one hit Ali's mother, she had just stumbled.

Adam also said in the interview he still hasn't been charged, but my lawyer has informed me, and I have seen the documents, that we are both facing charges in Beirut sometime in late September.

The next day Adam Whittington kept up his media campaign and spoke to broadcaster Alan Jones on his radio show. Again he presented as fact things that weren't correct but this time he dropped a bombshell that took my breath away. He said he had evidence that Col Chapman had tipped off Ali and was the reason the recovery was unsuccessful,

Lahela and Noah were taken from me again and we were all jailed. I've no reason to believe this is true, however at this point I don't know what to think. I do know that I now feel very wary.

With so much misinformation and misinterpretation of my story I am even more determined to put the record straight in these pages, for Lahela and Noah.

* * *

For readers who want the truth of how I feel, in my own words: I am devastated. I miss my two older children so badly some days that it hurts to breathe and I have to push through a heavy wall of grief just to get out of bed. If it wasn't for Eli and Brendan I possibly wouldn't try. But I am a mother who will never give up. Ali must realise I will not go away, and I will not stop asking to speak to and see my children. I want Lahela and Noah to know that too.

Chapter Thirty

Writing a book is a strange process, as is detailing the defining moments of a marriage. Seeing things in black and white makes me question the patterns of behaviour that weren't obvious at the time. When you are living through daily family life it is easy to ignore the small moments or conversations that should concern you and the warning signs that are so obvious in hindsight. I am starting to see things more clearly now, and it has been a painful process.

I wish that the past year and a half was only a nightmare and that I could wake up and it would all be over. If only Lahela and Noah were with me, getting to know their brother Eli and hanging out together at Chipmunks. Sadly, that isn't going to happen.

At the time of writing this, it has been three months since I returned to Australia. A lot has happened during that time. There has been a lot of coverage in the media about Channel Nine. The network held an internal inquiry into the role of *60 Minutes* in the recovery of Lahela and Noah, and the findings were highly critical of the decision to undertake the story. As a result, Stephen Rice lost his job. As I have said before, Stephen, Tara and the team helped me when no one else would, so I will never criticise any of them. And Tara helped me stay sane in prison; without her, it would have been unbearable.

All the noise around Channel Nine's involvement meant that Lahela and Noah's voices were lost. I cannot understand why the media did not focus on the fact that our laws and our government were powerless to stop Ali from keeping our children from me.

In late May 2016, Judge Abdullah handed down his findings in Lebanon: *60 Minutes* was fined a minimal amount for its role in the recovery, while Adam Whittington, his three CARI colleagues and I were charged with kidnapping. Adam was released on bail in July and finally made it home to his family. As of right now, September 2016, only Mohammed remains in jail. I hope he is released very soon and can return to his family. Every day I live with the knowledge that it all turned out so wrong. I still don't know how it did. Maybe I never will. All I know is, my family is broken.

My kidnapping charge means there is yet another barrier between me and the chance of seeing Lahela and Noah again. I am waiting to hear the trial date. I face seven years in prison, which terrifies me. I want so much to return to see Lahela and Noah, but I can't risk being imprisoned again and losing all three of my children. Eli is growing so quickly and needs his mum just as much as Lahela and Noah do. The only reason I face prison is because I was pushed into a desperate situation by a man who, I believe, made up his own laws.

I am a private person. I hate that my life and my children's lives have been laid bare. However, telling our story is so important because I need Lahela and Noah to know the truth. I want so very much to go back in time and stop Ali from getting on that flight with our children. People often say that domestic issues should be sorted out behind closed doors, but despite it all I am glad that my battle with Ali is now public and that I have told my story in this book, because not only do I want my children to know the truth, I want everyone to understand what others in similar situations may be going through. The broad issue of child custody and rights needs more attention from our lawmakers, and I can only hope that my story has alerted people in power to this.

No child deserves to be kept away from a caring, loving parent. I know that for sure. When a marriage or relationship breaks down between two adults, it is all too easy for the children to become pawns in a horrible game. We should never do that to our children. Sometimes, when a family breaks apart, there is the assumption that a child is better with one parent than another. I firmly believe – and always have – that a child will benefit more if they have meaningful contact with both parents, provided those parents have all good intentions of doing the best for their children and will keep them safe. As much as a child may be happy, healthy and seemingly well looked after by only one parent in a broken relationship, there is the chance that the child carries emotional scars that will be unlocked somewhere, sometime. That is my biggest fear about Lahela and Noah. Yes, I have contributed to this, but I genuinely believe that I was – and still am – seeking a healthy solution that will only benefit my children. I continue to wonder if Ali really wants the same.

The longer he stops me from speaking to them or seeing them gives me a very clear idea of his intentions.

When I went to Beirut to bring Lahela and Noah home, I could never have predicted the events that followed, nor the enormous public reaction. Since the recovery, I have learned a lot about how we judge others. I was condemned in some parts of the media – including social media – and by members of the general public for what I did. *How could she put her children in danger? How could she have put them through so much trauma?* My answer to this may also come in for harsh judgment, but I would be weak if I didn't say it. I know in my heart and mind that Lahela and Noah would be happier now if they were living in Australia. And I stress that I would not prevent Ali from visiting them, making contact with them, or indeed taking them back to Lebanon for holidays if he legally guaranteed he would bring them back to Australia again and the Lebanese courts made sure that occurred. If I had the children with me now, Lahela and Noah would have the chance to be guided through their formative years by *both* parents. However, right at this moment they are children without a mother. I know they need me. I saw the sadness in their eyes when their father shut that car door. Lahela knew that was the last time she would see her mum.

Ali has not upheld his very public assurances that I would be able to see the children. I have not been able to Skype or ring them. Recently, I was contacted by a friend of Ali's who told me Ali was only withholding contact because I was 'playing games' and wouldn't give him their immunisation booklets. I know that Ali had these booklets with their passports when he left Australia, but to avoid any confusion, I went to our family doctor and had their full immunisation records printed out, stamped and signed by the doctor, and then sent them to Ali. I didn't want him to have any excuse to keep me from Lahela and Noah. I haven't heard anything since, and I still haven't been allowed to make contact with the children. I value my children too highly to play games.

The most recent memories I have of Lahela and Noah are the pictures and photos that I have from our final time together in the McDonald's playground. Yes, Ali did send me the pictures I took that day. And he did so via Maggie within hours of leaving the playground. But since then there has been no communication. Embassy staff have tried to talk to him and he has turned them away. So, for those who wish to judge me and pass comment, may I say this: every parent going through a similar situation to mine is unique, and none of us should be prematurely condemned for trying our hardest to do what is best for our children.

Living without my two older children will never be easy. People are kind and they say things like, 'Time will help.' It won't. They say I must have hope. I do. I have to hold onto hope, because not to is far too bleak.

My dad told me I had to stay strong – and he is right. I must find the strength to keep standing and to keep fighting. Most of the time I can, but at the moment it isn't easy, and sorrow can hit at any time, in any place. While staying at Brendan's parents' home the other night I woke suddenly at 1am with an overwhelming sense of grief. It struck so hard, it made me recoil. Brendan was lying beside me and Eli was in the room too, both asleep. I sat up in bed and felt like I couldn't breathe. My chest hurt. I felt like the walls

331

and roof were pressing down on me and I was overwhelmed with the need to run. I dragged on shoes and stepped out the back door. I was crying and I ran, not knowing where I was running to. I ran hard and ended up at a waterway. I wanted to die. I'm not proud of this moment or even these emotions, and I feel weak and vulnerable revealing this. But in that instant I just wanted the extreme sadness to end. I wanted to enter the water and sink. I wanted to stop everything.

I don't know how long I stood there, but just as I was about to enter the water I felt someone grab me. Bear-hug me. I hoped it was someone who would take my life. It wasn't. It was one of the only people I have left who keeps me going. It was Brendan. He held me as I cried and screamed and sobbed until I was exhausted. I think he was scared to let go of me, so we just stood like that for a long time. Eventually he guided me back home, and the next day I was not so wretched.

If you see me laugh or joke or chat at the local shops, it means it is a good day. But regardless of my outward demeanour, Lahela and Noah's absence is always there. Sometimes it is the noises I don't hear – their laughter, their voices, the sound of their running feet or their cries for me – that are so loud they drown out everything else. Too many times lately I have found myself writing on the steamed-up shower screen at home the words 'come home to mummy', as I sob until I can barely breathe. I have to shake off the utter helplessness I feel and pull myself together – for Brendan and Eli.

I know that this is a long road I am on, that Lahela and Noah are on, and the horrible truth is that Ali only wins if I give up. I won't do that. I have to live my life as best I can and enjoy the joyful moments with Eli and Brendan. I look forward to telling Eli about his older brother and sister and making sure he knows all about them.

I will not let Ali destroy me. His manipulation and abuse is wrong. But Ali Elamine underestimates me. I am stronger than he knows. I can see now that he did the only thing he could do to really hurt me. And that reveals his weakness. One day Lahela and Noah will know that.

I feel that current international laws facilitate the type of behaviour displayed by Ali. He and others have escaped punishment for damaging the lives of children. I know I am a decent human being and a loving mother who would give my own life to guarantee the good health and happiness of all three of my children. Sadly, at this very moment, I have failed with Lahela and Noah. Ali has ignored legal orders and kept my children from me, and he has gotten away with it. To me, that means there has to be an enormous hole in various legal systems. Obviously that is a simplistic statement, but I am looking at it from the perspective of a parent who simply wants her children back. Child custody and abduction is an issue that needs to be urgently addressed. Long after my story has faded from the public's imagination, there will be two forgotten children. Not forgotten by me, my family, or my friends, but what about the policymakers and law-makers whose responsibility it is to ensure we have societies in which we can have faith? This is a difficult problem to fix, but it needs to be addressed. We must all look after our children. If we fail to do this, what does that say about us as human beings and our treatment of more generations of broken children?

It almost kills me to know that it is likely I won't see Lahela and Noah again until they are at least young adults and can make their own choices. By then, I hope they haven't been turned against me. I hope Ali and his family don't tell them I abandoned them, or did not want them, or replaced them. None of that would be the truth. I don't want to wait fifteen or twenty years to get a knock on the door. That is so wrong. Take just one example: nearly every parent remembers the first school day of their child's life. I've already missed that with Lahela. It will never come again.

All I am left with right now are memories. Rubbing Noah's feet at bedtime. The birthmark shaped like Tasmania on the sole of Lahela's left foot. The songs, the scooting, the sandcastles at the beach. I am not being sentimental by holding onto these so tightly; they help me get through every day. Whereas other parents can collect new memories day in and day out, mine are trapped in the past. They haunt me, yet they also give me strength.

I don't know what I will do from here. I know I am not okay, but step by step I have regained some degree of normalcy in my life. I am back working at a childcare centre and I'm still chipping away at the units for my Bachelor of Secondary Education. I want to have a career that my children will be proud of. My friends and family continue to support me, and we all share the same hopes.

Finally, I am determined to relish the joy of having a cheerful baby boy, and a loyal, loving partner with whom to share and raise him. I hope the sorrow that can overwhelm me will stay manageable because I am determined I will always be there for them both. And determined to be here when Lahela and Noah return to me.

Fourteen thousand kilometres away, my estranged husband is looking after our children. Ali, if you ever read this book, I want you to know that I feel sorry for you. You have messed me up, and you have tangled the lives of two innocent little people in ways that are inexcusable. I hope that one day soon you realise what you have done and make it right.

And to my beautiful Lahela and Noah, I can only imagine how much you are growing. One day, we will be together again. Until that moment, don't forget that Mummy will always love you. Mummy will always be here, waiting for you to come home.

Acknowledgments

To my family: life has been incredibly arduous the past year and a half, and if I didn't have you all and your endless flow of positivity I think my world would be a much darker place. My battle is your battle, we fight together. Brendan, thank you for saying those words to me that day, I really needed to hear it. I know you love my children the only way you know how to love – wholeheartedly and selflessly. Mum, Dad, your wise but stern words were heard with love that day and started my fire to fight again. Grandma, I remember the look on your face when you saw Lahela, your first great-grandchild on that day she was only hours old and I knew then and there how special a grandparent's bond is – my only hope is that you have a chance to tell them how much

336

you love them again before the time passes too quickly. Lew, Simon, Bryce, my quiet but loyal supporters, you are what kept Mum going. Barb, Greg, thank you for being the incredibly loving people I saw you were towards Lahela and Noah and the grandparents I know you are by looking after Eli back in Australia when I couldn't. Shane, thank you for helping your brother read through the legal minefield he was abruptly thrust into when everything turned horribly wrong. Courtney, Scott, your unconditional kindness and genuine need to know we were all doing okay meant a lot. Donna and Gary, Mum needed your support and it meant the world to know she found it in both of you. All of my mum's close friends – we are blessed to know you!

To all my friends who have shown their support and have tried tirelessly to help me give my children a voice, I thank you. A separate mention to Sacha and Dana; no matter the time of day or night you always answer my phone calls, even when you know they will be filled with tears and for that you have etched a special place in my heart forever. Jess, your random thoughtful gifts that would arrive in the mail throughout the year brightened my days just that little bit. Hannah, a wonderfully kind-hearted woman, you organised such a fabulous fundraiser that in turn helped me get the ball rolling legally – boy, you know a lot of people!

My legal team, *60 Minutes*, CARI, I can't thank you enough for giving me the hope of seeing my children again when even hope was running out. Tara, Stephen, Ben, Tangles and Kirsty, you have the kindest of hearts and I thank you for your words of encouragement, hugs and endless smiles. Tara, you will forever be my cell sister! Kirsty, thank you for being the ears who listened to my desperate words during those many stressful conversations – they kept me calm in those hours I would have probably otherwise fallen apart in. Sallie, I'll always remember you taking my hand in Sydney airport as we walked through the back exit avoiding media; just that simple gesture will be stuck in my mind for this lifetime. Ghassan and Dr Kamal, when I met you both in person for the first time I felt assured we were in good hands – you fought hard, and your constant updates gave us daily hope in trying times.

Maggie and Pascal, thank you for your reading material. I didn't fight Tara over some of those books you gave us to read, and I must admit I didn't read half as many as Tara did, but the ones I did read gave me a small sense of escape when I felt I was quickly losing all control. Having you both sitting with me as I saw my children for the last time at the playground helped me keep it together for them. P.S. You are extremely strong women!

Constance Hall – the Queen who said the many words I wished I could have said when I returned to my home country and to so much personal misrepresentation. To all my loyal and devoted followers via social media – a huge virtual hug and kiss from me! You all spent hours searching the World Wide Web on my behalf for any organisation, photo or avenue that might help my situation or lift my spirits. You all made a bigger difference than you will ever know.

And last but by no means least, Kathryn, Vanessa and James! My three musketeers. Without the three of you this book for my children to read in years to come would not have been possible. Three words that sum you all up: honest, kind and genuine. It's been a privilege to have met you all.

To my children: thank you for being you – it is an honour to be your mummy.

If you find yourself in difficulty, or reading this book makes you feel depressed or overwhelmed, there are people who can help.

Lifeline
www.lifeline.org.au or 13 11 14

Kids Helpline
kidshelpline.com.au or 1800 55 1800

beyondblue
www.beyondblue.org.au or 1300 22 4636

MensLine
www.mensline.org.au or 1300 78 99 78

Headspace
www.headspace.org.au or 1800 65 08 90

Family Court of Australia National Enquiry Centre
www.familycourt.gov.au/wps/wcm/connect/fcoaweb/contact-us/ or 1300 352 00

Eeny Meeny Miney Mo Foundation
www.emmm.org.au

An independent, not-for-profit organisation working:

- To protect children from the severe risks that arise during and after family separation.
- To ensure that children's rights and needs – especially to maintain a proper relationship with all loving parents, relatives and friends after family separation – are widely understood, protected and observed.
- To help those experiencing, or at risk of suffering, the tragic consequences of 'parental alienation'.